Dark-bellied Brent Goose
Branta bernicla bernicla
in Britain
1960/61 – 1999/2000

Robin M Ward

with contributions from
Rob Cameron, Denice Coverdale, Conor Donnelly, Barwolt Ebbinge, Chris Gibson, Bob Howells, Roy King, Bob Lord, Anne de Potier, Peter Potts, David Price, Carol Reid, Andrew St Joseph and Derek Wood

The Wildfowl & Wetlands Trust, Slimbridge, Glos GL2 7BT, UK

WWT

JOINT NATURE CONSERVATION COMMITTEE

Waterbird Review Series

ISBN 0 900806 47 8

This publication should be cited as:

Ward, RM. 2004. *Dark-bellied Brent Goose* Branta bernicla bernicla *in Britain 1960/61 – 1999/2000*. Waterbird Review Series, The Wildfowl & Wetlands Trust/Joint Nature Conservation Committee, Slimbridge.

Published by:

The Wildfowl & Wetlands Trust
Slimbridge
Gloucestershire
GL2 7BT

Joint Nature Conservation Committee
Monkstone House
City Road
Peterborough
PE1 1JY

T: 01453 891900
F: 01453 890827
E: research@wwt.org.uk

T: 01733 562626
F: 01733 555948
E: communications@jncc.gov.uk

Design and typeset by Paul Marshall and Beth Nightingale
Cover design by Pyneapple

Printed by Crowes Complete Print, 50 Hurricane Way, Airport Industrial Estate, Norwich, Norfolk NR6 6JB

Front cover: Dark-bellied Brent Goose by Chris Gomersall
Back cover: Thames Estuary (England) by Chris Gomersall

CONTENTS

Summary   v

1	**The Dark-bellied Brent Goose**	**1**
1.1	Introduction	1
1.2	Background	1
1.3	Monitoring and population assessment	1
	1.3.1 Counts	1
	1.3.2 Productivity	3
	1.3.3 Ringing	3
	1.3.4 Population assessment	3
1.4	Annual cycle	4
	1.4.1 Breeding season	4
	1.4.2 Autumn migration	5
	1.4.3 Winter	6
	1.4.4 Spring migration	9
1.5	Conservation and management	10
	1.5.1 Legislation and other conservation measures	10
	1.5.2 Hunting	12
	1.5.3 Agricultural conflict	12
2	**Survey of wintering areas**	**15**
2.1	England	17
	2.1.1 Northumberland	17
	2.1.2 Yorkshire & North Lincolnshire	18
	2.1.3 South Lincolnshire & North Norfolk	20
	2.1.4 Suffolk & Essex	21
	2.1.5 Thames & North Kent	30
	2.1.6 West Sussex	35
	2.1.7 The Solent	39
	2.1.8 Dorset	44
	2.1.9 Devon	48
2.2	Wales	48
	2.2.1 West Glamorgan & South Dyfed	48
3	**Future research needs**	**51**
4	**Acknowledgements**	**52**
5	**References**	**53**

SUMMARY

This review aims to assess changes in the abundance and distribution of the Dark-bellied Brent Goose *Branta bernicla bernicla* in Britain since winter 1960/61, to bring together available historical information prior to that winter, to review published data on the ecology and biology of this goose population, and to describe numbers, trends and site use at the key resorts in Britain.

The Dark-bellied Brent Goose breeds along the arctic coasts of the Yamal, Gydan and Taimyr Peninsulas and the islands of the Kara Sea. It winters exclusively along the coasts of Western Europe, the majority concentrated at sites along the Atlantic west coast of France, the south and east coasts of England, southwest Netherlands and the Wadden Sea. Migration takes place along the Western Palearctic flyway following the coastline from northern Russia, through the White Sea and Baltic Sea, and along the North Sea coast, the English Channel and the French Atlantic coast.

The first reliable population estimate for Dark-bellied Brent Geese was 15,000 in the winter of 1955/56. This census was undertaken during a period when the population level was very low: a decline in the 1930s followed a wasting disease and consequent reduction in levels of *Zostera*, the species' principal food resource. Hunting is, however, widely considered to have been the key factor responsible for the species decline at that time. During the 1990s, the Dark-bellied Brent Goose population increased and then fluctuated between approximately 220,000 and 315,000 individuals.

In Britain, the wintering population ceased growth in the late 1980s, and underwent a 16% decline within the period 1989/90 to 1999/2000. The latest estimate for the sub-species is Britain is 98,110 birds, around 33% of the world population.

On arrival in western Europe, favoured staging areas are the Danish and Schleswig-Holstein coasts of the Wadden Sea, and Foulness, Essex. From Foulness, birds disperse to winter in Britain as well as France from where birds may return in mid winter. Whilst most birds depart wintering sites in March for pre-migration fattening on the Wadden Sea, up to 10,000 birds now stage on the Wash and much smaller numbers use North Norfolk, North Kent, the Stour Estuary and the Beaulieu Estuary also.

Historically, the Dark-bellied Brent Goose was, and still is to some extent, a grazer of *Zostera*, *Enteromorpha*, and saltmarsh plants during the winter.

Since 1973, associated with the rapid growth in numbers, this population has, in Britain, begun to make extensive use of inland habitats for foraging, including grassland, winter cereals and oilseed rape. For most sites in Britain, there is a sequential pattern of habitat use as birds successively deplete *Zostera*, *Enteromorpha* and finally saltmarsh food resources prior to switching to foraging inland. By mid winter, a large proportion of feeding time is spent inland. Most birds return to saltmarshes to exploit fresh growth of more natural foods at their spring staging sites in Western Europe.

In England, conflict with agriculture arises in Norfolk, Suffolk, Essex and on the south coast where there have been cases of damage to crops of winter cereals and oilseed rape. To lessen the conflict locally, nature reserves are managed for these birds, providing alternative feeding areas often in combination with scaring operations outside. Although certain agri-environment schemes have the potential to provide incentives to tolerate Dark-bellied Brent Geese on appropriately managed farmland, none has yet realised this potential.

Five-year mean peak counts for 1995/96-1999/2000 identified that nine sites in Britain were of international importance for Dark-bellied Brent Goose (supporting at least 3,000 birds) and a further 17 were of national importance (holding 1,000 or more). Over the same time period, these sites in combination supported virtually all the Dark-bellied Brent Geese in Britain, all of which are designated as Special Protection Areas. Numerically, by far the most important sites for Dark-bellied Brent Goose are The Wash, Thames Estuary, North Norfolk Coast, Chichester Harbour and Blackwater Estuary. Information on numbers, trends and site use at the key resorts is provided within this review.

An International Single-Species Action Plan for the Dark-bellied Brent Goose has been prepared under the auspices of the African-Eurasian Waterbird Agreement and provides a framework for the conservation and management of this population.

Future research should focus on the incorporation of on-going surveillance programmes within a national Integrated Population Monitoring programme for the species. The monitoring of reproductive performance and survival rates of Dark-bellied Brent Geese is essential to ensure that fluctuations in population size are interpreted effectively and to provide an early warning of impending changes in population size.

1 THE DARK-BELLIED BRENT GOOSE

1.1 Introduction

In winter 1955/56, when the first reliable census was undertaken, there were an estimated 15,000 Dark-bellied Brent Geese *Branta bernicla bernicla* in the world (Salomonsen 1958). This number had increased to 315,000 birds by the 1990s with the dynamics and consequence of this increase the focus of much demographic and foraging ecology research, not least driven by the concerns from increasing usage of agricultural land by the geese (Ebbinge 1992, Ebbinge *et al*. 2002). Much of this work has been expertly reviewed by Ebbinge *et al.* (1999) in *Goose Populations of the Western Palearctic.*

Although well studies, much information on this population of geese has been published piecemeal, or is hidden in the form of internal reports or unpublished databases. In an attempt to collate information from Britain, this report aims to assess changes in the abundance and distribution of Dark-bellied Brent Geese since winter 1960/61, to provide current estimates of population size and to review our knowledge of the ecology of this goose.

This report is split into two main sections and follows the format of recent monitoring reviews produced, or in preparation, for geese and swans (e.g. Fox *et al*. 1994). The first section provides a review of our current knowledge of the ecology of this population of Dark-bellied Brent Geese. This information provides a backdrop against which the monitoring information can be viewed. In addition, gaps in our knowledge are highlighted, as are the conservation threats that face this population of geese.

The second section presents monitoring data on a regional scale from winter 1960/61 to 1999/2000. Spatial and temporal changes in abundance, and distribution are examined. Annual maxima and monthly peak counts are illustrated for internationally and nationally important sites.

1.2 Background

The nominate race of the Brent Goose, the Dark-bellied Brent Goose, is the most numerous of the three sub-species globally, and until recently had increased markedly in number from a population low in the 1950s. Its breeding range covers the coasts of the Yamal, Gydan and Taimyr Peninsulas and the islands of the Kara Sea, including Severnaya Zemlya (van Nugteren 1997). In winter it is a bird exclusively of the coasts of Western Europe, the majority concentrated at sites along the Atlantic west coast of France, the south and east coasts of England, southwest Netherlands and the Wadden Sea (Fig. 1; Cramp & Simmons 1977). Migration takes place along the Western Palearctic flyway, following the coastline from northern Russia, through the White Sea and Baltic Sea, and along the North Sea coast, the English Channel and the French Atlantic coast (Bergmann *et al.* 1994).

The Dark-bellied Brent Goose is principally a grazer on intertidal *Zostera* beds and saltmarsh during the non-breeding season. However, at some localities in recent years, there has been increasing use of agricultural land for foraging that has led the birds into conflict with landowners.

1.3 Monitoring and population assessment

1.3.1 Counts

The first systematically organised survey of Dark-bellied Brent Goose was in Great Britain in 1947 with the initiation by The Wildfowl Trust of the National Wildfowl Counts. Wetland sites were counted on the middle Sunday of the month by a network of volunteers, initially during the period September to March. From 1969, the Birds of Estuaries Enquiry ran in parallel, the two schemes eventually combining efforts to form the Wetland Bird Survey (WeBS). Indexing techniques have been specifically developed which allow between-year comparisons of these data. A full explanation of this indexing process is given in Prys-Jones *et al.* (1994), Underhill & Prys-Jones (1994) and Kirby *et al.* (1995). The Dark-bellied Brent Goose is one of the best monitored species by WeBS, because the scheme covers all sites regularly used by the species in Britain.

For most estuarine sites, and therefore those frequented by Dark-bellied Brent Goose, WeBS Core Counts occur at high tide. In order to establish and update information on site usage over the low tide period, the WeBS Low Tide Count Scheme was initiated in the winter of 1992/93.

Figure 1. Breeding, wintering and flyway ranges of Dark Bellied-Brent Goose *Branta bernicla bernicla* (adapted from Lack 1986, Madge & Burn 1988, Scott & Rose 1996, Snow & Perrins 1998 and Ebbinge *et al*. 1999).

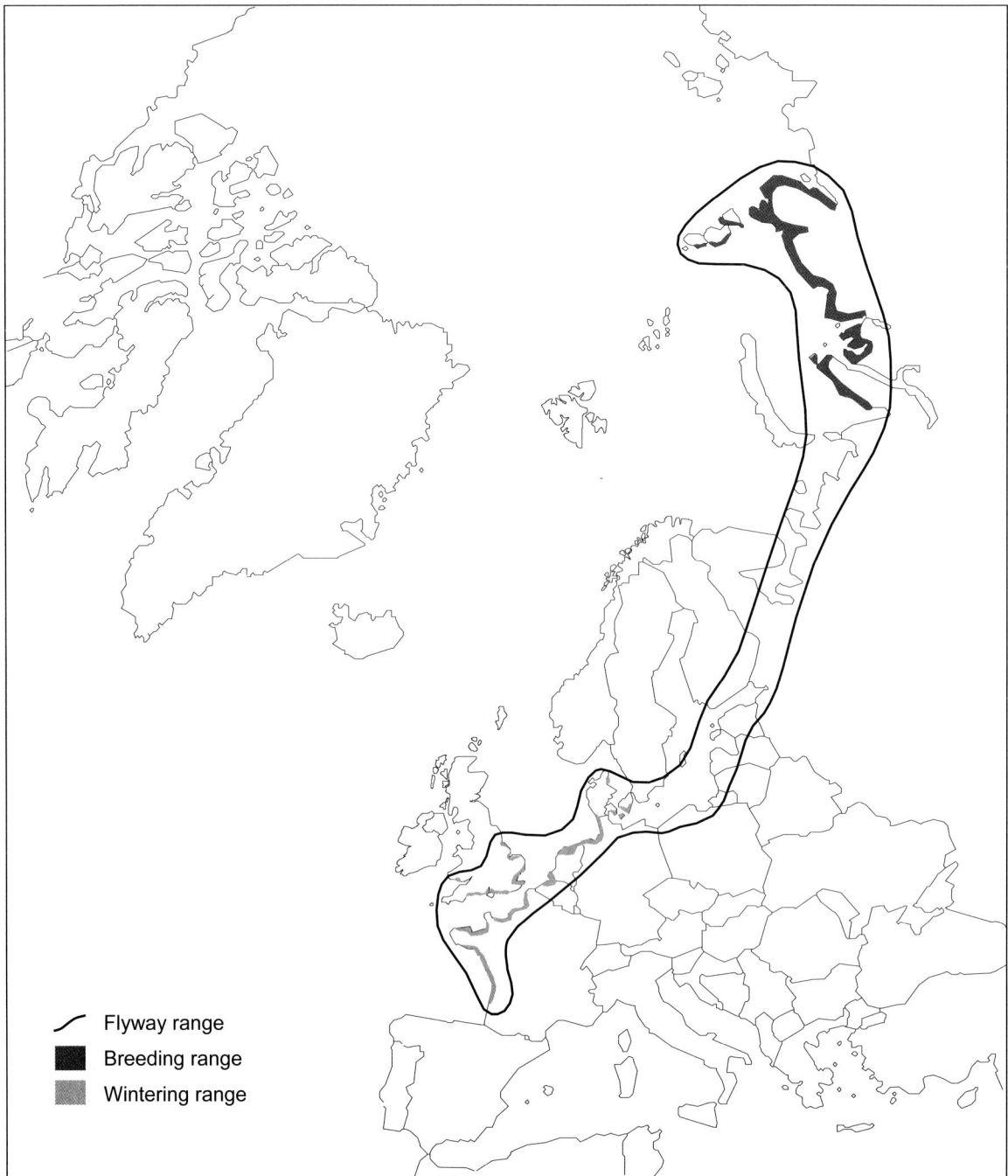

Monthly low water counts are undertaken through a winter period, with most individual estuaries surveyed about once every six years.

Following the creation of the International Waterfowl Research Institute (latterly IWRB, and now Wetlands International) in 1947, a mid winter (January) international waterfowl census was started in the mid 1950s. This census covered Dark-bellied Brent Geese. The need to co-ordinate, standardise and store data centrally has seen this on-going census develop under the auspices of the Goose Specialist Group of Wetlands International and it is now co-ordinated internationally by the Institute for Forestry and Nature Research (IBN-DLO) in Wageningen, the Netherlands. In this central database, count information is stored at three levels – site, national & international. With respect to the Dark-bellied Brent Goose, the annual precision of the population estimate is thought to be within 10% of the real total. Furthermore, a second international census now takes place in May when the majority of the population is less dispersed globally and, therefore, more accurately censused.

1.3.2   Productivity

An assessment of breeding performance, by recording the proportion of juveniles in autumn and winter flocks, has been systematically undertaken in Britain, the Netherlands and France. Juveniles are separable from adults by their upperwing coverts being tipped off-white (Mullarney *et al.* 1999). Internationally, these data are gathered under the auspices of the Goose Specialist Group. In Britain, this surveillance project, organised by the Wildfowl & Wetland Trust (WWT), has been on-going since 1985 and involves experienced voluntary observers determining brood sizes within flocks during late September to March (Hearn 2002).

1.3.3   Ringing

Ringing has been a key tool in identifying the network of sites that populations of migratory birds depend upon during the annual cycle. The catching and ringing of Dark-bellied Brent Geese began in Western Europe during the 1960s. Andrew St Joseph undertook a major ringing programme in Britian during the 1970s, this soon followed by ringing in the Netherlands, Germany and France. Closer to their Russian breeding grounds, ringing of Dark-bellied Brent Goose finally got underway in 1989 with birds caught and marked on the moulting grounds during late July and early August (Prokosch 1995). Cannon netting has been the principal

technique used to capture birds for ringing during the non-breeding season.

Between 1973-1993, almost 10,000 Dark-bellied Brent Geese had been ringed, half of which were ringed with metal rings only, and 5,022 with large engraved plastic leg rings only. The latter rings, designed to be legible in the field, had yielded no fewer than 134,812 re-sightings by 1997, with many re-sightings of the same individual throughout the flyway. These individually identifiable colour-ringed birds are providing a greater insight into site loyalty and turnover, family relationships, breeding success and longevity (Mitchell & Ogilvie 1997). Colour-ringing has demonstrated the great variability in migratory behaviour within one and the same population (Ebbinge & St Joseph 1992). The success of engraved colour-rings in facilitating recoveries is evident given that only 67 recoveries were generated from the 966 geese metal-ringed under the British ringing scheme up to the end of 2000 (Clark *et al.* 2002).

1.3.4   Population assessment

In the latter half of the 19th century, Salomonsen (1958) stated the number of Dark-bellied Brent Geese wintering in Europe must have amounted to about 216,00 birds.
Others have arrived at different conclusions when using the same data, suggesting the population size was lower (Atkinson-Willes & Matthews 1960). Whichever, the Dark-bellied Brent Goose had been common along the coast of Western Europe with a distribution linked to its preferred food resource, the vast intertidal beds of eelgrass (*Zostera* spp.) which then existed. In the 1930s, a wasting disease decimated *Zostera* beds across the globe and led to a crash in the Dark-bellied Brent Goose population across its range. In the Netherlands, birds attempting to switch to foraging inland on grassland and winter wheat were reportedly shot in large numbers (Ebbinge *et al.* 1999). Therefore, hunting may have been the key factor responsible for the species decline at that time. A marked change observed in the rate of increase in the population in 1972 coincided with a hunting ban in Denmark, adding more evidence that hunting limits population size (Ebbinge 1991).

It was during the period of extremely low population size that the first realistic estimate of the world's population of Dark-bellied Brent Geese was made, about 15,000 birds in winter 1955/56 (Ebbinge *et al.* 2002). During the 1990s, the Dark-bellied Brent Goose population increased to, and fluctuated at, between approximately 220,000 and 315,000 individuals (Fig. 2). As previously mentioned, after a slow initial population increase in the 1950s, a marked increase in the rate of change occurred in 1972. This was accompanied by a range expansion: in the UK northwards from their south and east England strongholds and inland onto fields causing increasing amounts of agricultural damage. By the 1980s, evidence for the levelling off in population size due to density dependence was proposed, but was later challenged on statistical analysis (Summers & Underhill 1991). Now, with the incorporation of data from the 1990s, the most recent demographic studies indicate that density dependence in reproduction or survival will result in the population levelling off (Ebbinge *et al.* 2002). Furthermore, it is predicted that the world population is likely to remain below 330,000. If correct, then the opportunity exists for governments and conservation bodies to plan for refuges to accommodate this size of population. These findings also provide some reassurance to farmers that further substantial increases in the subspecies with the associated economic losses are unlikely. The dynamics of the Dark-bellied Brent Goose population is complicated by the fact that there is a more or less tri-annual cycle of breeding success, the mechanism for which is discussed later.

In the UK, Dark-bellied Brent Geese numbers levelled off in the late 1980s, and have now undergone a 16% decline within the period 1989/90 to 1999/2000 (Gregory *et al.* 2002a; Fig. 3). The latest estimate of the number of Dark-bellied Brent Goose visiting Britain is 98,110 birds, 32.7% of the world population (Gregory *et al.* 2002b, Kershaw & Cranswick 2003). The assessment of breeding performance of this population from within Britain suggests, in eight of the last ten years, annual productivity has been below the estimated rate of mortality (15%) (Summers & Underhill 1991, Hearn 2002). Fig. 4 shows the proportion of young and mean brood sizes recorded in flocks of Dark-bellied Brent Goose in Britain since 1985. An unknown variable is the influence of 'short-stopping' (i.e. the wintering of birds closer to the breeding grounds), on demographic assessments in Britain (Hearn 2002). A reduction in the rate of reproduction is, however, evident across the wintering grounds in Europe (Ebbinge *et al.* 2002), with fewer pairs breeding but the productivity of these pairs having not altered. The availability of suitable nesting habitat is considered the main limiting factor, but other factors cannot be excluded (Ebbinge *et al.* 2002). In particular, food availability on spring staging sites is known to influence breeding performance, as does adverse weather during spring migration (Ebbinge 1989, Ebbinge & Spaans 1995).

1.4 Annual cycle

1.4.1 Breeding season

Range
The Dark-bellied Brent Goose breeds mainly along the coasts of the Taimyr Peninsula from 73° to 79° N, and from 75° to 122° E (Syroechkovsky & Zoeckler 1997). They are also reported to breed further north from Severnaya Zemlya (de Korte *et al.* 1995), further west from the Yamal Peninsula (Filchagov & Leonovich 1992), and a few breeding records have come from the Kanin Peninsula (Vinogradov 1994). The sub-species range has extended eastwards with population growth, as confirmed by the discovery in 1997 of a mixed colony of Dark-bellied Brent Geese and Black Barnt *B. b. nigricans* in the Olenyok Delta, west of the Lena Delta (Syroechkovsky & Zoeckler 1997).

Phenology
Dark-bellied Brent Geese begin arriving in the core breeding areas from the second week of June with egg laying usually underway within a week, before the snow and ice has thawed (Clausen 1997, Spaans *et al.* 1998). Within 100 days of arrival, the adults and their broods leave the breeding grounds between mid August and the first week in September.

Habitat
The breeding grounds of the Dark-bellied Brent Goose extend across the lowland tundra of the north Siberian coast. It encompasses the steep slopes of hills not higher than 100 m above sea level, river valleys and coastal plains (van Nugteren 1997). Nesting occurs on small islands, in extensive low-lying river deltas, dispersed along many small streams on the mainland tundra and on more the remote offshore islands with extremely poor vegetation (Spaans *et al.* 1993, Ebbinge *et al.* 1999). Large moulting concentrations of non-breeders occur on the numerous lakes, streams and branches of deltas of the lowlands (van Nugteren 1997).

Breeding Ecology
The Dark-bellied Brent Goose population more or less follows a tri-annual cycle of breeding success which involves a complete breeding failure every third year, followed by seasons of poor then variable breeding success. The principal driver of this cycle is the variability in predator pressure upon the geese on the breeding grounds as consequence of the three-year cycle in lemming abundance and associated predators (Summers & Underhill 1987, Spaans *et al.* 1998). The numbers of Arctic Foxes *Alopex lagopus* and Snowy Owls *Nyctea scandiaca*, which feed primarily on lemmings *Lemmus sibiricus* and

Dicrostonyx torquatus when available, increase markedly in peak lemming years. Following a peak lemming year, the proportion of first winter Dark-bellied Brent Geese on the wintering grounds has been 5-50%, and on average 29%. The following year, the lemming population having collapsed, both predators are forced to range more widely in search of both lemmings and alternative prey, including Dark-bellied Brent Geese. In these years, Dark-bellied Brent Geese always fail to rear substantial number of young; the proportions of first winter birds following such years have been below 7%, with the mean at 1% (Ebbinge *et al.* 2002). At such times, Dark-bellied Brent Geese will forgo breeding when Arctic Foxes are present during nest initiation; disturbance rather than increased predation by Foxes is now suggested to be the mechanism for widespread breeding failure of these geese (Spaans *et al.* 1998). The third 'unpredictable' year of the three-year cycle is regularly one of poor breeding success for the Dark-bellied Brent Goose, but can be good with up to 50% of winter flocks comprising juveniles.

Dark-bellied Brent Geese nest, most colonially, at comparatively low densities (maximim 3.9 nests/ha) due to defending large territories around the nest where the female forages during incubation (Cramp & Simmons 1977, Spaans *et al.* 1993, van Nugteren 1997). The largest concentrations of breeding Dark-bellied Brent Geese occur on small islands within gull colonies (both Herring Gull *Larus argentatus* and Glaucous Gull *Larus hyperboreus*; Spaans *et al.* 1993), or on very remote offshore islands, with much lower numbers dispersed over low-lying delta areas. These are the least accessible areas to predatory Arctic Foxes, due to the surrounding water and extensive ice sheets, the risk of venturing out to such sites only taken in years of low lemming abundance (Spaans *et al.*1998). For those birds nesting within gull colonies, the gulls provide additional protection against Snowy Owls as well as against other gulls (Ebbinge and Spaans 2002). In addition, through fertilisation by their droppings, the gulls indirectly provide nesting birds with high quality grass during the incubation period (Ebbinge and Spaans 2002). Mainland nesting areas are apparently only used when lemming numbers are high and predation from Arctic Foxes and Snowy Owls is low. In recent years, Dark-bellied Brent Geese have been observed nesting within the nesting territories of Snowy Owls where foxes are aggressively excluded (Summers *et al.* 1994, Spaans *et al.* 1998, Ebbinge & Spaans 2002). Dark-bellied Brent Geese will also occasionally breed on cliffs within the vicinity of other breeding raptors e.g. Peregrine *Falco peregrinus* and Rough-legged Buzzard *Buteo lagopus* (van Nugteren 1997).

Age of first breeding of Dark-bellied Brent Geese is 2 or 3 years. Clutches of 2-5 eggs are laid during mid to late June, incubation usually taking 24-26 days with most hatchings occurring during 10- 25 July (Spaans *et al.* 1993, Summers *et al.* 1994). During the first week after hatching, most broods are led away by the adults from island nest sites to food-rich river-banks and coastal areas of the mainland, the fledging period being c.40 days (Cramp & Simmons 1977, Spaans *et al.* 1998, Ebbinge & Spaans 2002).

Feeding Ecology
Dark-bellied Brent Geese arrive on the tundra as it clears of snow and ice, and feeding conditions locally are initially very poor. Little is known about feeding ecology on the breeding grounds. However, birds reportedly favour grassy tundra along the river valleys or near the coast, with monocotyledons (in particular *Poaceae* and *Cyperaceae*) contributing most to their diet (Cramp & Simmons 1977, van Nugteren 1997). Faecal analysis indicates that goslings feed more on insects and dicotyledons than do adults (van Nugteren 1997).

Moult migration and moulting areas
Many immature Dark-bellied Brent Geese do not migrate as far as the breeding grounds, instead gathering to spend the summer and moult either on the Kanin and Kola Peninsulas, Kolguuev Island or detour north to moult on the Novaya Zemlya Islands (Cramp & Simmons 1977, Bianki 1979, Kistchinski & Vronski 1979). Otherwise, large moulting concentrations of non-breeders occur within the lowlands and include the Niznyaya Taimyra Delta and Pyasina Delta, with up to 45,000 and 10,000 moulting birds respectively (Ebbinge *et al.* 1999). It is, however, only during years of poor productivity that moult migration is evident and then it is never large. Otherwise, sites such as Niznyaya Taimyra Delta have comparatively small moulting flocks, e.g. only 4,000 at Niznyaya Taimyra Delta, breeders moulting where and whilst rearing their brood to fledging

1.4.2   Autumn migration

Range
From their breeding grounds in the Taimyr westward, the Dark-bellied Brent Goose migrates along the arctic coast of Russia to the White Sea area, then overland to the Gulfs of Finland and Bothnia, and finally down into the Baltic Sea before arriving at their winter range (Cramp & Simmons 1977). The route is the reverse of that used in the spring though through a wider corridor (e.g. including Kolguiev islands) and with slightly different stopovers in the Barents Sea (van Nugteren

1997). Satellite tracking has not showed the use of a wider migration corridor in autumn, but those birds followed were non-breeding individuals and, therefore, not wholly representative (Green *et al.* 2002b). The White Sea and areas to the east are used as a stopover to refuel. Well known sites in the former include the west coasts of Onega and Dvina Bays (Bianki 1979). Migration overland to the Gulf of Finland goes via Lake Ladoga (Lampio 1979), with onward movement noted along the coasts of Estonia and Southeast Sweden where some birds cut overland over Skane (Fredga 1979). Small flocks stage in the Baltic Sea for a short time, in Estonia and on the island of Oland, Sweden (Ebbinge *et al.*1999).

Whereas some birds fly direct to their wintering grounds, others first stage along the Danish and Schleswig-Holstein coasts of the Wadden Sea (Madsen 1994, van Nugteren 1997). Here, most remain though the autumn prior to moving on to wintering grounds in England and France (Ebbinge *et al.*1999). England also hosts an important autumn staging site: the extensive intertidal flats off Foulness Island on the Essex coast (St Joseph 1979a). In Denmark, the largest flocks are found around Fanø and Rømø (Madsen 1994).

Phenology
Birds leave the Russian tundra breeding grounds from mid August through to early September and migrate west through the Kara Sea in early September (Biankii 1979). From mid September through to early October, birds pass through the White Sea area and staging sites such as Onega Bay (Biankii 1979, van Nugteren 1997) and on to the Gulf of Finland (Lampio 1979). Depending on the weather, birds may arrive on the Estonian coast by mid September where passage continues through to mid November following an October peak as noted further east in the Baltic Sea.
The first birds arrive on the Danish and Schleswig-Holstein coasts of the Wadden Sea from mid September, peaking during October (Madsen 1994, Rösner & Stock 1994). In Schleswig-Holstein, birds arrive earlier. Following a breeding season of low productivity, numbers remain high through the autumn in this area (Rösner & Stock 1994). Following a successful breeding season, the first flocks to arrive at the Wadden Sea contain few young, the proportion of first winter birds then increasing rapidly (Lambeck 1990). A marked decline sets in over mid winter as most families tend to move to sites further south.

Dispersal
In autumn, a component of the Dark-bellied Brent Goose population migrates direct to its wintering

quarters, whilst others stop off for the autumn on the Wadden Sea in Denmark and Germany. Most of the latter cohort subsequently moves on to the main coastal wintering grounds in England, France and the Netherlands.

Habitat
Intertidal mudflats are the most important habitat for Dark-bellied Brent Geese when staging at sites in the autumn, though some saltmarshes are also utilised, e.g. along the Schleswig-Holstein coast (Rösner & Stock 1994). At all staging sites, the birds roost on water in the intertidal zone.

Feeding Ecology
In the Danish Wadden Sea and White Sea area, staging birds forage almost exclusively on the mudflats, feeding on *Zostera* and *Enteromorpha* (Bianki 1979, Nehls 1979, Madsen 1994, van Nugteren 1997). Dark-bellied Brent Geese eat both the rhizomes and the leaves of *Zostera* on exposed mudflats and by upending in shallow waters (Rowcliffe & Mitchell 1998). Along the coast of Schleswig-Holstein, birds also graze saltmarsh plants (Rösner & Stock 1994).

1.4.3 Winter

Range
The Dark-bellied Brent Goose winters exclusively along the West European coast, the core areas being along the Atlantic west coast of France, the south and east coasts of England, the south-western parts of the Netherlands (Dutch Delta area) and in the Wadden Sea (Netherlands, Germany and Denmark).

During mild winters, birds are distributed throughout the Wadden Sea, with major concentrations along the Dutch coast and further to the south in the Dutch Delta area. During severe winters birds will leave the Danish and German parts of the Wadden Sea. Likewise, the 2,000 birds in the inner Danish waters, the Kattegat, will only remain through mild winters (Ebbinge *et al.* 1999). In England, the range extends down the North Sea coast from Lindisfarne in the north-east, along the English Channel coast and west to Cornwall in the southwest. Concurrent with the recent population increase, up to 1,200 birds now winter in south-west Wales coast at the Burry Inlet. The majority of birds wintering in France are found along the Atlantic west coast south to Bassin d'Arcachon, with birds also frequenting the northwest coast estuaries bordering the English Channel. The Channel Islands support up to 1,500 birds (Musgrove *et al.* 2001)

Phenology
The first birds arrive on the wintering grounds from mid September in the Wadden Sea and by the end of September in England (Madsen 1994, Rösner & Stock 1994, van Nugteren 1997). On the Wadden Sea, numbers peak in October with those remaining in the Danish and German parts, up to 10,000 birds, leaving during January and February for England and France when winters are severe (Ebbinge *et al.* 1999). In the Dutch parts of the Wadden Sea, numbers may reach as high as 44,000 birds during mild winters (Ebbinge *et al.* 1999). Further south in the Dutch Delta, numbers peak in November with large numbers remaining through the winter until March, some birds having moved to sites in England and France (van Nutgeren 1997).

In recent years, the number of birds visiting Britain has peaked at 74,000–101,000 birds, usually after November, following immigration from the continent and particularly during severe winters (Musgrove *et al.* 2001). From November, the group of up to 17,000 birds that concentrates in autumn on Maplin Sands, off Foulness, Essex, disperses to other east coast sites, the English south coast and France, after *Zostera* stocks have been depleted (St Joseph 1979a). In the 1970s, the increased numbers of birds in southeast England in autumn led to the establishment of new overland migration routes between Foulness and the south coast for those individuals wintering in West Sussex and France (Harrison 1979).

The arrival of the first wintering Dark-bellied Brent Geese in France has advanced by 10-15 days (usually 15-25 September) since the 1980s (Ebbinge *et al.* 1999). Furthermore, the timing of the mid winter peak counts of up 17,000 birds on the north coast and 100,000 along the Atlantic west coast, have also occurred earlier in recent years (November) (Ebbinge *et al.* 1999). From autumn, birds concentrate at those sites important for *Zostera*, in particular the Golfe du Morbihan where up to 50,000 birds can gather in October. Following *Zostera* depletion at these sites, numbers decline slightly in January as some birds return to more northerly sites in England and the Netherlands. The majority of birds, however, spread out from these sites along the French coast, at which point Bassin d'Arcachon becomes the most important site where up to 38,000 birds occur. Most of these birds migrate northwards in late March.

Return migration to spring staging areas in the Wadden Sea from those wintering areas to the west and south starts from late February and the last geese leave during May (van Nugteren 1997).

Dispersal
Young birds generally winter further south than adults, perhaps a consequence of more favourable climate or more profitable foraging in southern France (Lambeck 1990). Colour-ringing studies have shown that the majority of Dark-bellied Brent Geese show a high degree of fidelity to and within autumn and winter sites between years (St Joseph 1979a). Furthermore, different sub-groups, as already described, exist within the wintering range (van Nugteren 1997).

Habitat
Historically, the habitats occupied in winter were exclusively intertidal, predominately mudflats and saltmarshes (Ranwell & Downing 1959, Charman & Macey 1978, van Nugteren 1997). From the early 1930s, birds were observed using pasture and arable land in the Netherlands, but only sporadically and in winter (van Nugteren 1997). Since 1973, over the period of rapid population growth, the population has, over much of its winter range, has made extensive use of inland habitats for foraging, including grassland, winter cereals and oilseed rape (St Joseph 1979b, Summers & Critchley 1990, van Nugteren 1997).

It is only in Denmark and France that the majority of birds now remain feeding in the intertidal zone throughout the winter (Ebbinge *et al.* 1999). Elsewhere, a sequential pattern of habitat use occurs during the autumn and winter, dependent upon local availability. Throughout the range in late autumn, the Dark-bellied Brent Goose remains exclusively a species of the intertidal zone, initially foraging across the intertidal flats, followed by the grazing of saltmarsh. Having depleted intertidal food resources by early winter at the majority of sites in Britain, the Netherlands and Germany, birds now spend a large proportion of their total daylight feeding time inland (e.g. Summers & Critchley 1990). This is particularly notable along the south coast of England, where the extent of suitable intertidal habitat is generally more limited than on its east coast (Rowcliffe & Mitchell 1998). Regardless of the intensity of feeding inland, the birds remain dependent upon the intertidal zone as a safe haven to roost at night.

Feeding Ecology
In winter, Dark-bellied Brent Geese will preferentially feed on *Zostera* and then green algae (*Enteromorpha* spp. and *Ulva* spp.) on the intertidal flats and in low-water channels. When tidal inundation floods *Zostera* and algal beds, birds may then continue foraging during high tide on saltmarsh (Summers & Critchley 1990). In the 1930s, a wasting disease decimated the *Zostera* beds across Western Europe (Rowcliffe & Mitchell 1998). More recently,

further declines in *Zostera* abundance have been noted with the anthropogenic factors currently limiting re-establishment (Rowcliffe & Mitchell 1998, Ebbinge *et al.* 1999). Across much of the range, depletion of *Zostera* and then green algae now occurs by early winter when birds. As a consequence, birds first move on to saltmarsh and then, once saltmarsh plants have been depleted, on to agricultural land. The timing and extent of this sequential pattern of habitat use during the autumn and winter is dependent upon local availability of food resources.

Denmark and France, as mentioned earlier, are the only two countries where sufficient stocks of *Zostera* and *Enteromorpha* still remain to enable the majority of Dark-bellied Brent Geese to feed intertidally throughout the winter (Ebbinge *et al.* 1999). Where extensive areas of *Zostera* still remain in England, e.g. Lindisfarne and the Exe Estuary, this intertidal habitat is still the most important foraging area for wintering birds. By contrast, in Norfolk, beds of *Zostera* and green algae are now very limited in extent and the relatively extensive saltmarshes now provide the most important intertidal habitat (Rowcliffe & Mitchell 1998).

In autumn, low saltmarsh dominated by the annual *Salicornia* spp. is used extensively by Dark-bellied Brent Geese, the seeds of *Salicornia* and the leaves of *Aster tripolium* providing the main food resources here (Summers *et al.* 1993). The availability of this resource is, however, limited to a few weeks in October and November, providing only a minor contribution to the overall winter grazing of this habitat (Rowcliffe & Mitchell 1998). Dark-bellied Brent Geese also select the leaves of the succulent halophytes *Triglochin maritima* and *Plantago maritima* in the autumn.

For much of the winter when grazing saltmarsh, Dark-bellied Brent Geese prefer the high saltmarsh with a low-growing plant community dominated by the grass *Puccinellia maritima*, with those areas frequented most having a much higher proportion of the vegetation type known as 'lavender green' (Rowcliffe *et al.* 1995). The latter is composed of short, relatively species-rich swards where the main plant species are, in order of abundance: *Limonium vulgare, Puccinella maritima, Armeria maritima, Triglochin maritimum* and *Plantago maritima*. Since grass forms the main food resource here, its re-growth allows the habitat to be used throughout the winter. Some areas of saltmarsh are subject to cyclic grazing patterns by Dark-bellied Brent Geese, optimising the nutrient quality of this resource (Rowcliffe *et al.* 1995). Whether a suitable saltmarsh habitat is grazed cyclically may be influenced by disturbance, position

in relation to roost and inland feeding, and the occurrence of night-feeding (Rowcliffe *et al.* 1995).

At many sites by late October/early November, Dark-bellied Brent Geese will have started to feed inland, usually initially on winter cereals (Summers & Critchley 1990, McKay *et al.* 1994). By mid winter, a large proportion of total feeding time is spent inland at most sites in Britain, this equating to 74% of the day (dawn–dusk) during January to March for the North Norfolk coast flocks (Summers & Critchley 1990). Diurnally, the geese will move onto the fields sometime after dawn, the timing dependent upon the tide, the birds initially feeding on saltmarsh when available. Field width and distance from the sea influences which fields are used (McKay *et al.* 1994). Departure from field feeding is usually by mass flighting shortly before dusk to intertidal areas where birds generally roost at night. Some night feeding may occur over high water when birds are able to swim from a roost directly on to saltmarsh, this totalling approximately two hours of feeding time on the North Norfolk coast (Rowcliffe *et al.* 1995). As early as November, birds will switch from winter cereals to pasture, as observed at Chichester and Pagham Harbours (Round 1982, Summers & Critchley 1990, McKay *et al.* 1994). This habitat shift is though to be related to the birds' nutritional requirements changing over the winter, from high levels of protein to high levels of carbohydrates (McKay *et al.* 1994).

Though there is some evidence of a switch back to cereals before spring migration (McKay *et al.* 1994), the main habitat shift that occurs by mid March is the return to intertidal habitats, initially saltmarsh (Prop 1997). This occurs for most birds with their relocation to spring staging sites in western Europe, principally the Wadden Sea (Prop 1997).

In Essex, where numbers of Dark-bellied Brent Geese have declined in some areas by as much as 50% over the past decade, the close proximity of fresh drinking water is considered a major factor influencing the selection of feeding areas (A. St. Joseph & D. Wood pers. comm.). Outfalls, streams, rivers, farm reservoirs, fleets, borrow-dykes, gravel pits, storm drains, floods even large puddles may all be utilised. Elsewhere in the non-breeding range, birds foraging on saltmarshes fly to inland water sources, suggesting again that freshwater may well influence habitat use (Stahl *et al.* 2002).

1.4.4   Spring migration

Range

From late January onwards, and especially from March, most Dark-bellied Brent Geese return to the Wadden Sea, a spring staging site (van Nugteren *et al.*1997). Distribution within the Wadden Sea is centred upon the Dutch and Schleswig-Holstein coasts with much lower numbers in Niedersachsen. Comparatively low numbers of birds, 5,000-8,000, stage in spring outside the Wadden Sea along the Danish coast and the Baltic coast of Germany (Nehls 1979). A recent development, possibly a result of the population growth, has been the staging of birds in the Dutch Delta, with up to 10,500 birds, and in Britain, notably on The Wash and North Kent Marshes with up to 14,000 and 3,500 birds respectively (Ebbinge *et al.* 1999). Elsewhere in Britain, the Stour Estuary and Beaulieu Estuary now suppport up to 500 birds until late May (P. Potts & D. Wood pers. comm.).

The spring migration route is the reverse of that used in the autumn though using a narrower corridor of some 20-300 km width (van Nutgeren 1997). From its wintering grounds in Western Europe, the Dark-bellied Brent Goose migrates through the Baltic Sea, on through the Gulf of Finland to cross overland to the White Sea at Onega Bay (van Nutgeren 1997). Migration continues across the White Sea, crossing the Kanin Peninsula between Shoyna and Nes. From here birds proceed east along the arctic coast of Russia, rarely deviating far from it, before arriving at their breeding grounds in the Taimyr (Cramp & Simmons 1977, Green *et al.* 2002a).

When crossing the Baltic, the majority of Dark-bellied Brent Geese bypass staging areas in Denmark and Germany, flying direct from the Wadden Sea to those staging areas in the White Sea, these being principally the archipelago on the west coast of Onega Bay, Unskaya Bay on the west coast of Dvina Bay and the Dry Sea on the east coast of Dvina Bay (van Nugteren 1997). To the east, another major staging area is the southern part of the Kanin Peninsula (van Nugteren 1997). The results of satellite telemetry studies suggest that several short stops are made by the birds en route to the White Sea, each lasting an average of 9.5 hours, the purposes of which are considered to be for drinking and resting (Green *et al.* 2002a).

Phenology

Spring migration is well underway by early March with most birds having left England and France by mid April to stage on the Wadden Sea (St Joseph 1979a, van Nugteren 1997). Here, numbers in the Dutch and German (mainly Schleswig-Holstein) parts peak in April and May, the peak in Danish waters being slightly later. Elsewhere, gatherings at the recently developed staging areas in the Dutch Delta and in England, The Wash and North Kent Marshes, peak in mid May. The main departure period from these staging areas is the latter half of May with only stragglers left after mid June. Adverse wind conditions can, however, delay departure for the White Sea, the next principal staging area; in the Wadden Sea this can be as late as the last days in May (Ebbinge 1989).

The staging period for the geese in the White Sea is late May, with most birds stopping over for 3-5 days before departure around 1 June, depending on arrival date (Clausen 1997). From there it is thought that the birds' next leg is to the Kanin Peninsula where they stage for a further week on the tundra (Clausen 1997). Mass spring migration of these geese across the Kanin Peninsula occurs during 10-14 June (Ebbinge & Spaans 1995, Green *et al.* 2002a). Birds eventually begin arriving on their breeding grounds during 10–20 June, with peak passage at Yugorsky Shar Strait being 8-15 June (Ebbinge & Spaans 1995, Clausen 1997).

Dispersal

It has been suggested that the majority of birds wintering in France and Britain migrate to spring stopovers in the Netherlands, Germany and Denmark (St Joseph 1979a).

Habitat

The seasonal pattern of habitat use by Dark-bellied Brent Geese during the spring, is the reverse of that observed in the autumn and early winter (Prop 1997). By mid March, most geese have returned to intertidal habitats to forage, initially saltmarsh, the switch for most birds coinciding with their relocation to spring staging sites in western Europe (Prop 1997). The timing of this habitat switch is influenced by the weather and its impact upon the development of new growth of saltmarsh vegetation. Growth of *Zostera* and algae is often limited prior to departure of Dark-bellied Brent Geese from western Europe, with the species relying primarily on saltmarsh during the spring fattening period. It is later, when staging in the White Sea, that the majority of geese revert to using intertidal flats, where *Zostera* is the most important food resource (Clausen 1997). In the Baltic, however, birds feed intertidally on *Zostera* throughout the spring (van Nugteren 1997). Further east, when staging on the southern Kanin Peninsula, birds forage primarily on the tundra.

Locally within the Netherlands and Denmark, the saltmarsh resource has been unable to support the larger numbers in recent years, with some birds now regularly foraging on improved pastures in spring (Madsen 1994, van Nugteren 1997).

Feeding Ecology
The sequential pattern of use of the different habitats by Dark-bellied Brent Geese in spring corresponds to the phenology of new growth (Prop 1997). Saltmarsh vegetation starts growing later in the season than the inland grasses, the switch back to saltmarsh grazing coinciding with this new growth. The selection of plants resuming growth after winter hibernation is thought to be the consequence of enhanced digestibility and nutrient quality, enabling rapid fattening prior to migration (Props 1997, Rowcliffe & Mitchell 1998). In search of this fresh growth, the preferences shown for different saltmarsh food plants changes during the season with the succession of new growth (Prop 1997). Thus, during April and May, when most Dark-bellied Brent Geese are foraging on saltmarsh, the main foods are successively *Festuca rubra, Puccinellia maritima,* and *Plantago maritima,* with *Triglochin maritima, Aster tripolium* and *Salicornia* spp. The cyclical grazing of saltmarsh, as described earlier for the wintering grounds, also occurs on the spring staging sites (van Nugteren 1997).

The body reserves laid down by Dark-bellied Brent Geese on the spring staging grounds of the Wadden Sea, are considered inadequate to enable them to then migrate the full distance to the Taimyr Peninsula (Ebbinge & Spaans 1995). It would seem that the White Sea is a necessary refuelling area where the most important food resource is *Zostera* (Ebbinge & Spaans 1995, Clausen 1997). Further to the east on the southern part of the Kanin Peninsula, staging birds forage mostly on the tundra (van Nugteren 1997).

1.5 Conservation and management

1.5.1 Legislation and other conservation measures

1.5.1.1 International

Conservation status
In BirdLife International's Species of European Conservation Concern, the Brent Goose is classified as a SPEC 3 species which means that it has an unfavourable conservation status in Europe, but is not concentrated in Europe. The population is also listed under Category B (2) b and c of the African-

Eurasian Waterbird Agreement (AEWA), prepared under the Bonn Convention on Migratory Species, because there are more than around 100,000 individuals in the population that are considered to be in need of special attention as a result of dependence on a habitat type which is under severe threat and showing significant long-term decline.

Habitat protection
The EC Directive on the conservation of wild birds requires Member States to classify Special Protection Areas (SPAs) for this migratory species. I Britain, the SPA suite comprises 19 sites where the Dark-bellied Brent Goose has been listed as a qualifying species, supporting on average 93,677 individuals between them and representing94% of the British population (Stroud *et al.* 2001). Further international protection of important wetlands habitats for Dark-bellied Brent Geese is provided through the Ramsar Convention on Wetlands of International Importance especially ass Waterfowl Habitat and through the Bern Convention on the Conservation of Wildlife and Natural habitats 1979.

Away from Britain, the breeding areas in Taimyr fall within the protection of reserves although the active conservation management in these areas is often not enacted. There is no known protection of sites in the White Sea. Most internationally important sites in Denmark, Germany, The Netherlands and France benefit from strict protection under European legislation and the Ramsar Convention, translated through national instruments.

Species protection
General provisions of the EC Birds Directive apply within the European Union. The species is listed in Annex II of the Directive which restricts areas in which hunting may occur under national legislation. As a migratory species, the general provisions of the Bern Convention also offer protection. Away from Britain, the species is fully protected in the Taimyr, Denmark, Germany, Netherlands, and France, but not in the White Sea.

Other measures
An International Action Plan has been prepared for the Dark-bellied Brent Goose. The intention of this Action Plan is to fulfill the obligations of Range states under the AEWA. The general objective of the plan is to permit the Dark-bellied Brent Goose to attain an equilibrium population, taking into account habitat requirements of the species throughout the annual cycle, and human interests (e.g. farming, hunting, birdwatching etc.). The National Management Options/Actions for Britain, which are framed around the International Management Objectives, are summarised in Table 1.

Table 1. Draft AEWA International Single-Species Action Plan for the Dark-bellied Brent Goose: National Management Options for the UK

International objective	National management options/actions
A minimum disturbance of the species	• Establish, as necessary and appropriate, adequate disturbance-free refuge zones within protected areas through control of relevant potentially damaging activities.
Good quality habitats	• Maintain or enhance current status of habitats • Encourage appropriate management for natural and semi-natural sites of importance for Dark-bellied Brent Geese. Select and classify an appropriate national suite of EU Special Protection Areas for Dark-bellied Brent Geese. • Ensure appropriate management sites for protected areas. • Encourage Integrated Coastal Zone Management to reduce conflicts between Dark-bellied Brent Geese and other competing uses/users of the coast.
Sufficient extent of habitat	• Establish a national inventory of natural habitats of Brent Geese that are potentially threatened by sea-level rise. • Encourage the managed retreat of coastlines in areas where salt-marsh of importance to Dark-bellied Brent Geese is being, or will be, lost through rising sea-levels. • Encourage re-establishment of former feeding areas.
Reduction of conflicts with agriculture	• Establish disturbance-free refuge zones • Integrate management for Brent Geese by farmers with their own nature management activities at key sites with other 'wider countryside' measures on semi-natural habitats and farmland. • Apply Council Regulation (EEC) 2078/92 on agricultural production methods compatible with requirements of the protection of the environment. • Seek to integrate biodiversity objectives into the future reform of the Common Agricultural Policy and the development of future Community funding mechanisms. • Clarify political and financial frameworks and the desired objectives for Goose conservation by activities, so that farmers can execute their professional skills and responsibility with these ends in mind. • Produce advisory material for farmers and government officials on the opportunities for management of Brent Geese on agricultural land. • Establish local strategies for alleviation of crop damage in 'problem' areas. • Facilitate schemes of co-operation between farmers, e.g. scaring activities.
Population monitoring	• Collect annual monitoring data at site and national levels and provide to international collations.

1.5.1.2 Britain

Conservation status

The Brent Goose appears on the 'Amber' list of the 'Population Status of Birds in the UK, Channel Islands and the Isle of Man' because 20% or more of the Northwest European Brent Goose 'population' occurs in the UK during the non-breeding season, 50% or more of the UK non-breeding 'population' can be found at ten or fewer sites and because it has an unfavourable conservation status in Europe (SPEC 3) (Gregory *et al.* 2002b).

Habitat protection

The key site designation for Dark-bellied Brent Geese in Britain is Site of Special Scientific Interest (SSSI). Guidelines for the selection of sites have been formally published by the Nature Conservancy Council in 1989 under the title Guidelines for the selection of biological SSSIs. National Nature Reserves (NNR) are areas of national and sometimes international importance which are owned or leased by the appropriate statutory conservation body, or bodies leased by them, or are managed in accordance with Nature Reserve Agreements with landowners

and occupiers. NNRs are also classified as SSSIs and attract similar protection. Legislative protection for these sites derives from the Wildlife & Countryside Act 1981. Under these provisions operations likely to damage the nature conservation interest of SSSIs are subject to control.

Species protection

General protection is afforded under the Wildlife & Countryside Act 1981. Where agricultural damage is serious, the Department for Environment, Food & Rural Affairs (DEFRA) currently issues licences under the Wildlife & Countryside Act 1981 for the killing of birds when no other satisfactory solution is available. The licences are solely intended to re-enforce scaring for the purpose of preventing serious damage to crops (Barrett 2002).

Dark-bellied Brent Geese have been fully protected in Britain since 1954. During prolonged periods of severe winter weather, legislation requires the suspension of hunting that may alleviate disturbance of birds at a time when the birds are most likely to be constrained energetically.

1.5.2 Hunting

Under the terms of the African-Eurasian Waterbird Agreement of the Bonn Convention, the size of the Dark-bellied Brent Goose population is such that it allows the possibility of sustainable hunting. The Dark-bellied Brent Goose is currently listed on Annexe II (2) of the EU-Birds Directive so under Article 7 the subspecies can be hunted only in accordance with national legislation. The draft International Action Plan calls for an extensive study on the effects of hunting on this population and a feasibility study on the setting up of bag limits for each country. The draft Action Plan does, however, state clearly that 'the culling of Dark-bellied Brent Geese in not a suitable management option for a reduction in the size of the Dark-bellied Brent Goose population'.

1.5.3 Agricultural conflict

The development of inland feeding has lead the Dark-bellied Brent Goose into major agricultural conflict in the UK, parts of the Wadden Sea, and the south-western part of the Netherlands (Summers & Critchley 1990, Salmon & Fox 1991, McKay *et al.* 1994, Vickery *et al.* 1995). In France, of the few sites where Dark-bellied Brent Geese do resort to grazing small areas of grasslands and winter cereals in late winter, it is only in the Baie de Bourgneuf where this has actually resulted in conflict with agriculture (Maheo 1994, Ebbinge *et al.* 1999). For the remaining parts of the non-breeding range, agricultural damage is not a major issue. In Niedersachsen (Germany), the Baltic, and Denmark, regardless of season, inland feeding by Dark-bellied Brent Geese on crops or grassland is uncommon, whereas birds staging in the White Sea feed principally on *Zostera* and occasionally on saltmarshes (Madsen 1994, Potel & Sudbeck 1994, Clausen 1997, van Nugteren 1997).

In Britain, conflict arises in Norfolk, Suffolk, Essex and the south coast where severe damage by Dark-bellied Brent Geese can begin from late autumn onwards on winter cereals and oil-seed rape crops, whilst the impact upon permanent pasture is considered to be very low. Around parts of the Wadden Sea and Southwest Netherlands, the agricultural conflict is focused on damage to grassland, seed-culture and winter wheat. This conflict is the consequence of wintering birds encountering a reduced area of *Zostera* on which to forage in recent years and/or the available preferred saltmarshes being unable to support the existing numbers in spring (Ebbinge 1992).

Grazing of arable by Dark-bellied Brent Geese does not appear always to cause crop damage as grazing can lead to tillering which leads to more heads on shorter straw, giving a similar yield overall (C.Gibson *in litt.*). In some parts of south Essex, grazing of winter linseed has been suggested as beneficial. In this case, grazing causes the production of more, smaller seed heads, with a greater total yield, and the seed are borne on shorter, less fibrous stems that are easier to combine (C.Gibson *in litt.*). Any damage to crops is more through the puddling effect of the feet, rather than grazing.

The most efficient and cost effective technique for scaring birds from crops has been demonstrated to be active scaring by a full-time human bird scarer (Summer & Hillman 1990, Vickery & Summers 1992). This approach is further enhanced when backed up by the shooting of small numbers of geese. In Britain, where no financial compensation is paid to farmers, licences are available to shoot Dark-bellied Brent Geese in order to prevent serious agricultural damage by scaring birds on to the alternative feeding areas provided. Under licence, about 1,000-3,000 Dark-bellied Brent Geese are shot in southeast England annually. This is under the annual limit of 4,000 set by DEFRA. Because scaring is reasonably effective, the main cost to farmers lies not in damage in crops but in scaring activities. To lessen the conflict locally between agricultural interests and Dark-bellied Brent Geese in the UK and Southwest Netherlands, agricultural land is managed for these birds, providing extensive Alternative Feeding Areas (AFAs). In these areas, grazing livestock are used to maintain an attractive grass sward for Dark-bellied Brent Geese. Often such alternative feeding areas are managed in combination with goose scaring operations outside the AFA, this being the most effective strategy when using scaring tactics (Ebbinge *et al.* 1999). Most existing AFAs are permanent pasture within nature reserves or SSSIs, the latter managed under the agreement of English Nature. Recent studies suggest a management prescription for AFAs of large, open, unfertilised short sward grasslands, sown with a high proportion of White Clover *Trifolium repens*, that are far from roads and paths but within 5 km of a roost site and close to the sea (McKay *et al.* 2001). The provision of AFAs is now recognised as the most promising and cost-effective way of managing the conflict between agriculture and Dark-bellied Brent Geese (McKay *et al.* 2001).

Although certain agri-environment schemes in Britain have the potential to provide incentives for the toleration of Dark-bellied Brent Geese on appropriately managed farmland (e.g. set-a-side or Environmentally Sensitive Areas), few have yet realised this potential (Rowcliffe & Mitchell 1998, C.

Gibson pers. comm.). This is because, as with the hierarchy of preference on tidal food sources, there has been a hierarchy inland with arable crops being preferred to grasses (C. Gibson pers. comm.). In this situation, grass will only be used where there is efficient scaring from crops. However, the recommendations from studies such as McKay *et al.* (2001) in seeking to switch the hierarchical gradient through improving the attractiveness of grassland AFAs, may help in avoiding or reducing the need for scaring. Perhaps the findings of the most recent demographic studies that predict further substantial increase in the subspecies as unlikely (Ebbinge *et al.* 2002), will also give confidence to land managers to plan a strategy to accommodate the current population on refuges, where necessary.

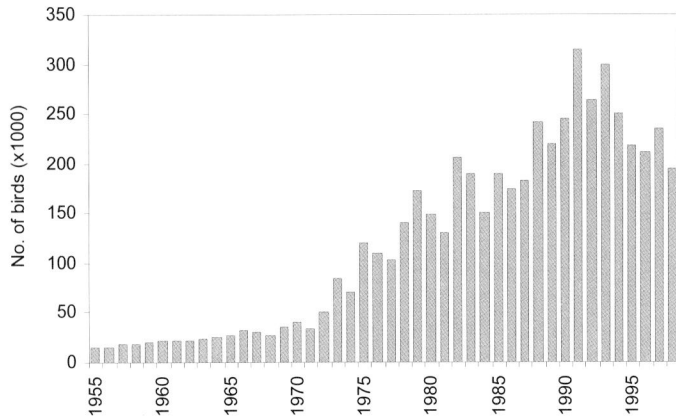

Figure 2. Global population estimates for Dark-bellied Brent Geese, 1955-1999 (Data source: Ebbinge *et al.* 2002)

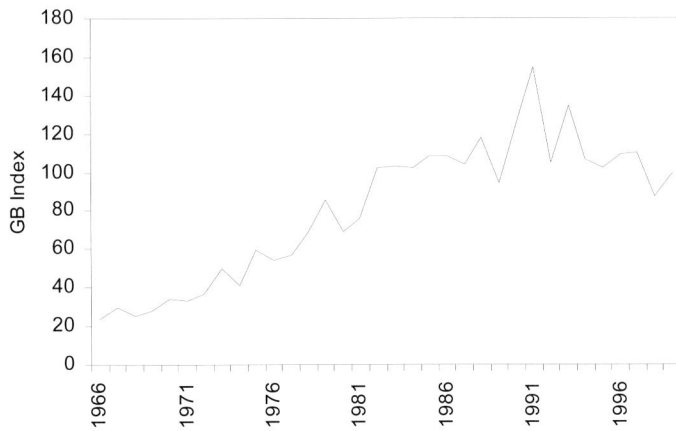

Figure 3. Annual index for Dark-bellied Brent Geese in Britain, 1966/67-1999/2000

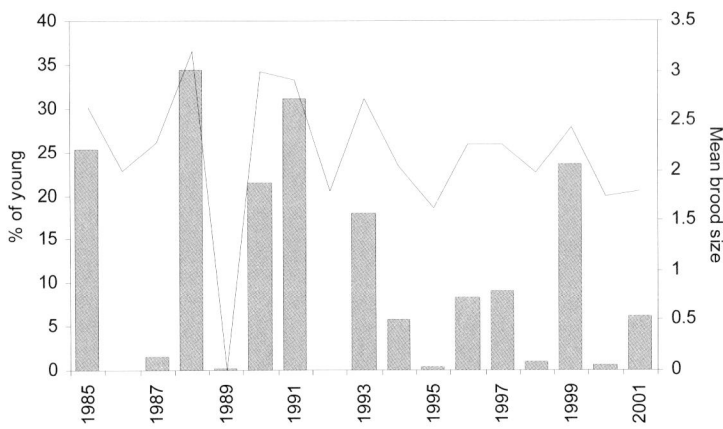

Figure 4. The proportion of young (bars) and mean brood size (line) of Dark-bellied Brent Geese in Britain, 1985-2000

2   SURVEY OF WINTERING AREAS

The following accounts provide a detailed review of the abundance, distribution and phenology of Dark-bellied Brent Geese wintering in Britain based on data collected through international and national monitoring schemes. Some counts were obtained from county bird reports or by regional experts. Geographically discrete regions of importance for wintering Dark-bellied Brent Goose are considered separately and split into the following sections:

Background
This section provides a brief overview of regional landscape and the availability of suitable habitat for Dark-bellied Brent Geese.

Historical status
Based primarily on data collected since 1960/61, this section provides an overview up to the present day of trends in numbers at a site-based and regional level. However, where published information is available, the status prior to 1960/61 is also reviewed. This section also highlights those sites that were once important for Dark-bellied Brent Geese but which have fallen in status over the review period.

Internationally/nationally important sites
Detailed accounts of internationally important sites are presented. Wetland sites are considered internationally important if they regularly support 1% of the individuals in the global population following the criteria agreed by the Contracting Parties to the Ramsar Convention on Wetlands of International Importance. A wetland in Britain is considered nationally important if it regularly holds 1% or more of the British population. Provisional assessments of importance are made on the basis of three years data, following the Ramsar Convention.

The threshold for international importance during the five-year period used for site assessment in this review is 3,000 birds (Rose & Scott 1997). However, international population estimates, and subsequent thresholds, are revised periodically and that for the Dark-bellied Brent Goose now stands at 2,200 (Wetlands International 2002). In line with accepted practice, this threshold has not been applied retrospectively and so some sites may not be listed in this review that may in future assessments meet the revised international threshold.

The threshold for national importance in Britain is 1,000 birds (Musgrove *et al.* 2001). Five-year mean maxima for each internationally and nationally important site in Britain are shown in Table 2.

The locations of each of these sites are illustrated in Fig. 5.

Table 2. Sites of international and national importance for Dark-bellied Brent Goose in Britain (in descending order of importance)

Site name	5-year mean (1995/96-1999/2000)
1. The Wash	22,874
2. Thames Estuary	12,913
3. North Norfolk Coast	10,812
4. Chichester Harbour	9,120
5. Blackwater Estuary	8,891
6. Hamford Water	6,829
7. Langstone Harbour	6,247
8. Crouch-Roach Estuary	4,539
9. Colne Estuary	3,762
10. Fleet/Way	2,580
11. Portsmouth Harbour	2,579
12. North West Solent	2,501
13. Medway Estuary	2,482
14. Deben Estuary	2,269
15. Southampton Water	2,200
16. Humber Flats, Marshes and Coast	2,184
17. Dengie Estuary	2,176
18. Swale Estuary	2,172
19. Pagham Harbour	2,133
20. Stour Estuary	1,973
21. Beaulieu Estuary	1,853
22. Exe Estuary	1,709
23. Newtown Estuary	1,514
24. Poole Harbour	1,441
25. Orwell Estuary	1,219
26. Burry Inlet	1,069

Site accounts contain detailed information on current status and trends, site protection measures, habitats present, and site use. For each site account, much of the information provided on habitats is drawn from the seven volume series *An inventory of UK estuaries* compiled by the Coastal Review Unit of JNCC's Coastal Conservation Branch e.g. Buck (1993). The reader is referred to these for further and more detailed site description information. For definitions of international site status and selection criteria/guidelines mentioned in the text, see www.english-nature.org.uk for SSSIs, Stroud *et al.* (2001) for Special Protection Areas (SPAs), Ramsar

Figure 5. The locations of sites of international importance and national importance for Dark-bellied Brent Geese in Britain (see table 2 for key to sites)

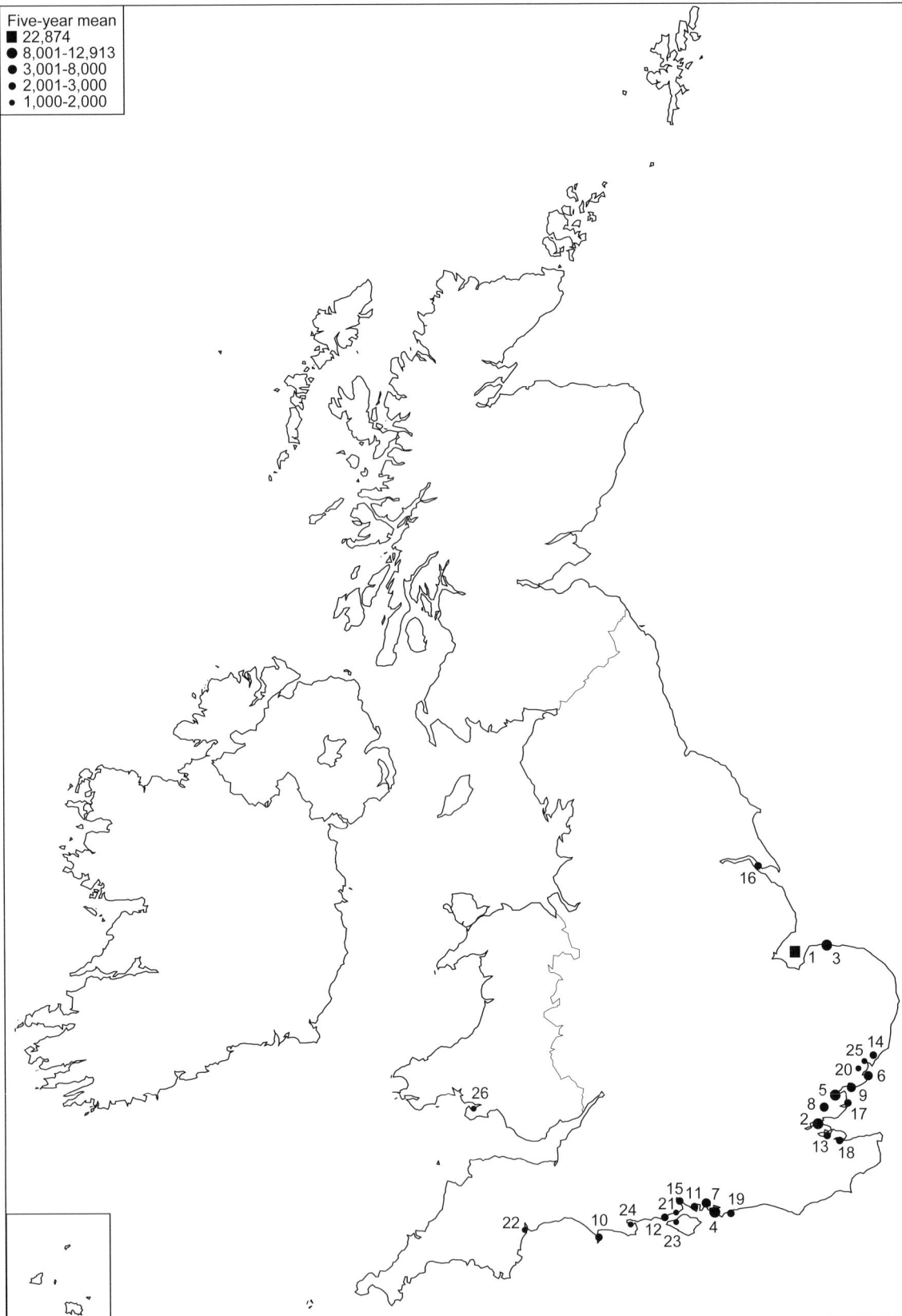

(1999) for Ramsar sites, and Heath & Evans (2000) for Important Bird Areas (IBAs).

Other sites
This section lists those sites which regularly support large flocks of Dark-bellied Brent Geese during peak times in the winter and/or which have a long history of occupancy but which do not support nationally or internationally important numbers according to WeBS.

Key references
This section provides a comprehensive list of relevant literature and published monitoring data on Dark-bellied Brent Geese in each region.

2.1 England

2.1.1 Northumberland

2.1.1.1 Background

The western half of Northumberland is dominated by the Cheviots, a landscape of open upland habitats and Kielder Forest. A sharp contrast is provided to the east by the lowland coastal belt of mixed agricultural, this abruptly changing to areas of urbanisation and industry in the south. Coalfields lie in the southern quarter, the footprint of the mining industry evident not least by a mosaic of wetland habitats as a consequence of subsidence. The eastern boundary is dominated by open coast habitats of sand beaches and dunes alternating with rocky scars and low lying cliffs. The coast's intertidal flats are essentially restricted to Lindisfarne (NU1041), the region's other five estuaries being small; their combined intertidal area less than 6% of the former locality.

Lindisfarne is one of only two barrier beach estuarine systems in the UK, encompassing the coastline from Cheswick south to Budle Bay where Holy Island is the 'barrier'. It supports one of the largest intertidal areas in northeast England with 2,713 ha of intertidal sand- and mudflats, and 218 ha of saltmarsh. Extensive beds of *Zostera* exist south of the causeway to Holy Island, in particular Fenham Flats, but it is absent from Budle Bay (P. Davey pers. comm.). The *Zostera* is however suffering saltmarsh encroachment aided by the invasion of the cordgrass *Spartina*. The landscape adjacent to the estuary is primarily large arable fields both on the mainland and to a lesser degree Holy Island where there are also extensive areas of pasture.

From their arrival, birds forage upon the extensive *Zostera* beds in the south, Fenham Flats. Since 1995 this has been supplemented at Lindisfarne for the much more numerous Light-bellied Brent Geese by feeding on winter cereals, from late December to March (Rowcliffe & Mitchell 1998). Given the mixing of these subspecies and identical feeding ecology, it is unsurprising that Dark-bellied Brent Goose also feed in fields (P. Davey pers. comm.).

2.1.1.2 Historical status

Historically, Lindisfarne has been the principal wintering site for the Svalbard/Northeast Greenland population Light-bellied Geese *B. b. hrota* and Dark-bellied Brent Geese in Northumberland. Prior to 1960, most of the regular wintering birds at Lindisfarne were thought to be Dark-bellied Brent Geese, the mixed race flock during 1875–1900 numbering no more than 1,000 (Atkinson-Willes & Matthews 1960). When cold weather influxes of Light-bellied Brent Geese from their Danish wintering grounds occurred, the flock size at Lindisfarne would then peak at up to 20,000 birds, as occurred in 1886 (Atkinson-Willes & Matthews 1960, Owen *et al.* 1986). The UK-wide decline of *Zostera* in the 1930s resulted not only in drastically reduced numbers of Brent Geese (both races) but also caused a major shift in distribution, with Northumberland declining in importance for Dark-bellied Brent Goose. Between then and the early 1950s, peak winter counts of Brent Geese (both races) at Lindisfarne rarely exceeded 100 birds. Since the 1960s, the vast majority of Brent Geese wintering in Northumberland have been Light-bellied, with Dark-bellied birds seen regularly but in very small numbers until the late 1980s (Fig. 6). This is in spite of stricter protection from wildfowling at Lindisfarne in the mid 1960s that led to a substantial increase in the numbers of most other waterbirds at this site (Owen *et al.* 1986).

In recent decades, the pattern of occurrence of Dark-bellied Brent Geese has been highly variable. Birds often arrive by October, numbers peaking at anytime between then and January. However since winter 1994/95 this pattern has altered, peak numbers now occurring during February or March in four of the five most recent winter periods (Fig. 7). This included an unprecedented influx of 517 birds in February 2000. The change in phenology has not been coincident with an increase in peak counts from 1988 onwards, although differences between years are often marked. The five-year mean for 1995/96-1999/2000 was 148 birds. The observed variability is consistent with the site acting as a refuge in cold weather and for birds otherwise displaced from sites at their carrying capacity threshold. Colour-ringing has identified that wintering birds in Lindisfarne stage on the Wadden Sea in March (Ebbinge *et al.* 1999).

2.1.2   Yorkshire & North Lincolnshire

2.1.2.1   Background

One of Britain's largest estuaries, the Humber Estuary, dominates this region. It stretches from Trent Falls at the confluence of the Trent and Ouse, 62 km eastwards to Spurn Head, a shingle spit that extends out into the mouth from the north shore. At the mouth on the north shore, the spit and shore profile combine to form an intertidal embayment of 13 km length, the otherwise relatively narrow estuary expanding at this point to a 7.5 km width. The major ports of Grimsby, Hull, Goole and Immingham together with the associated industrial complexes, though localised, dominate the estuary landscape along much of its length. A coastal plain of grazing and arable land otherwise flanks the estuary with the Lincolnshire Wolds rising to the south. Extending north of the Humber, the coast is of low-lying cliffs facing onto sandy beaches and offshore banks of coarse shingle. South of the Humber, a broad sandy beach flank the Lincolnshire coast to Skegness backed by saltmarsh and sand dunes.

2.1.2.2   Historical status

Although counts have been sufficient to assess Dark-bellied Brent Geese usage of the Humber since 1974 (Owen *et al.* 1986), there is no prior indication that an established wintering flock regularly used the Humber Estuary before then. From the mid 1970s, the *Zostera* beds within the shelter of Spurn Point became established as the focus of a small number of wintering Dark-bellied Brent Geese, initially numbering fifty or so birds (Fig. 8). From the late 1970s to the mid 1990s, this flock size increased at a rate greater than that observed in the population as a whole (Rowcliffe & Mitchell 1998). Numbers have since reached a plateau at the site, with peak counts fluctuating around a thousand or so birds.

2.1.2.3   Nationally important sites

i) Humber Flats, Marshes and Coast

Five-year mean 95/96-99/2000: 2,184

Site conservation status
SPA (Humber Flats, Marshes and Coast: selection stage 1.3)Ramsar (Humber Flats, Marshes and Coast, non-qualifying species)

NNR (Spurn, Saltfleetby-Theddlethorpe Dunes)
SSSI (various)
IBA (Humber Flats, Marshes and Coast: non-listed species)

Site description and habitat
The tidal range of the Humber Estuary (TA2020) is the second highest for any estuary in the UK. At low tide, the exposed intertidal areas comprise approximately one third of the estuary (13,521 ha) with sand and mudflats extending much of its length. 5,000 ha of this habitat is on the upper estuary above Barton. Downstream of Hull, the intertidal flats of the outer estuary become progressively wider and firm, with the 13 km stretch west of Spurn Point of major importance to waterbirds. The latter 2,400 ha of intertidal flats support occasional beds of *Zostera*. On the opposite bank of the outer estuary, a broad sandy beach backed by a dune system and saltmarsh stretches from Cleethorpes southwards along the coast to Theddlethorpe. The inner estuary supports extensive areas of reedbed (*Phragmites*) with areas of mature and developing saltmarsh backed by grazing marsh in the middle and outer estuary.

Numbers and trends
Numbers on the Humber Estuary typically peak in December or January (Fig. 9), with up to 2,500 birds present. Fewer than half of this number remain through to March, birds having relocated to fatten prior to migration. Prior to a re-assessment of the global population in the mid 1990s, and consequently the 1% criteria, the Humber Estuary was, for several years, identified as international important for Dark-bellied Brent Geese.

Site use
The intertidal flats of both sides of the outer estuary continue to be of much importance to Dark-bellied Brent Geese, with the majority located south of Donna Nook, along the coastline around Saltfleetby (Owen *et al.* 1986). Indeed, a WeBS Low Tide Count in the winter of 1998/99 found most birds concentrated at Gainsthorpe Haven with smaller numbers along the south shore up to Grimsby and at Spurn Bight (Pollitt *et al.* 2000).

Figure 6. Dark-bellied Brent Geese at Lindisfarne, 1960/61-1999/2000: peak counts (bars) and British index (line) (circles denote years with no known data)

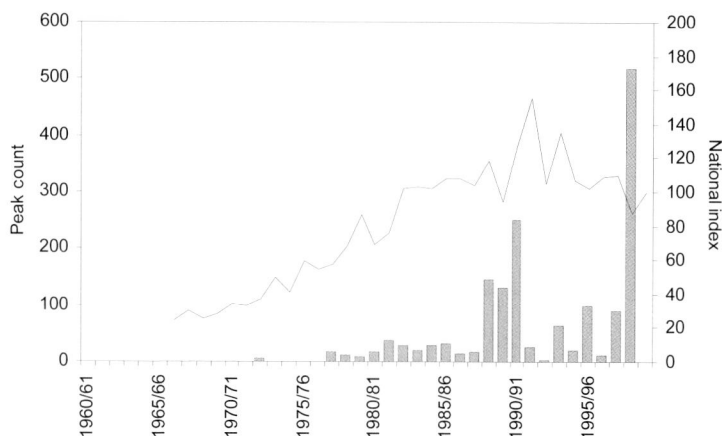

Figure 7. Dark-bellied Brent Geese at Lindisfarne, 1995/96-1999/2000: mean peak counts by month (error bars denote minimum and maximum peak counts during the period)

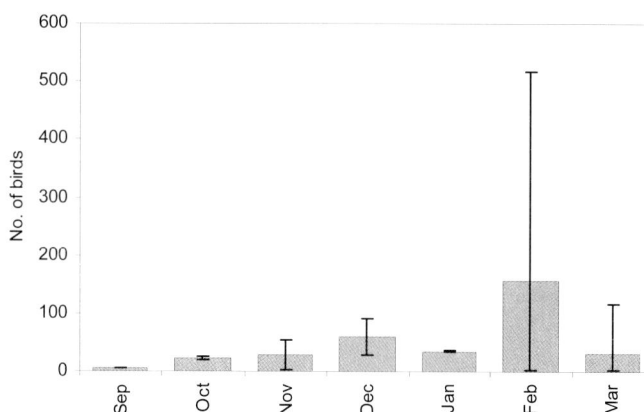

Figure 8. Dark-bellied Brent Geese at the Humber Estuary, 1960/61-1999/2000: peak counts (bars) and British index (line) (circles denote years with no known data)

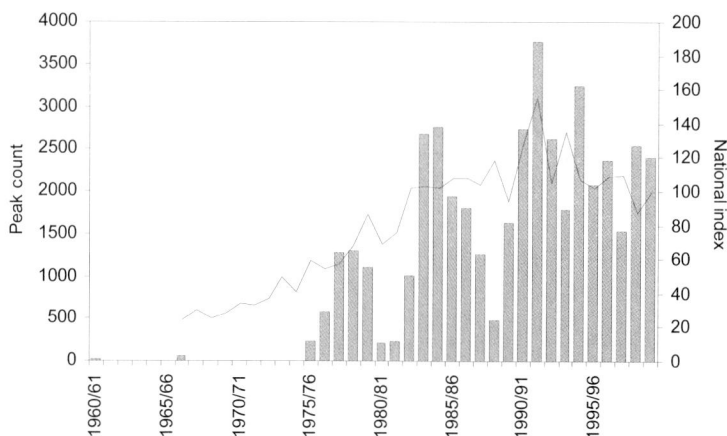

Figure 9. Dark-bellied Brent Geese at the Humber Estuary, 1995/96-1999/2000: mean peak counts by month (error bars denote minimum and maximum peak counts during the period)

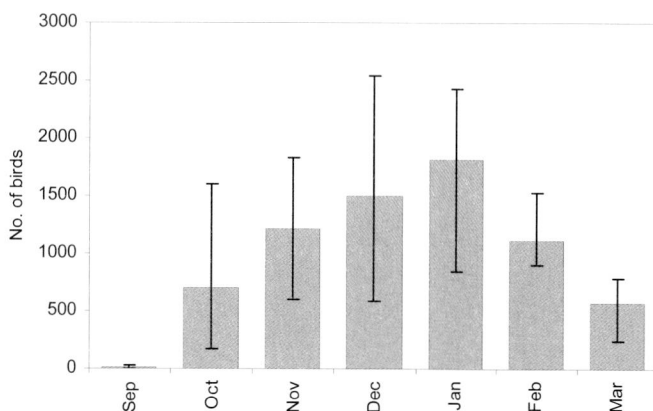

2.1.3   South Lincolnshire & North Norfolk

2.1.3.1   Background

Central to this coast is the UK's largest estuary, The Wash, a major embayment at the mouth of its four tributaries (Ouse, Nene, Welland and Witham). The Wash has one of the largest expanses of intertidal flats and saltmarsh in the British Isles.
This is despite much of the upper saltmarsh zone having been land claimed, this contributing to the much drained fenlands, now a flat exposed arable landscape criss-crossed by drainage ditches, much below sea level. This terrestrial landscape extents northwards of Gibraltar Point, a large sand dune system that marks the northern extremity of the Wash. A similar lip forms the adjacent corner at Holme, but against a mixed, more enclosed and undulating agricultural landscape that fringes the Wash east coast. Industry around the Wash is largely concentrated at the mouths of the tributaries, in particular the Ports of Kings Lynn and Boston. From Holme east to Cley, the North Norfolk coast exhibits one of the most diverse coastal systems in Britain. A series of small streams enter the sea through a complex contiguous zone of intertidal flats, saltmarshes, freshwater marshes, sand dunes, beaches, spits and islands.

2.1.3.2   Historical status

The North Norfolk Coast and the western shore of The Wash (Kirton to Wainfleet) have been the focus of the Dark-bellied Brent Goose range in this region. Increasing numbers of birds on The Wash, following *Zostera* die-back in the 1930s, led to the range expanding out from the western shore to other parts of the embayment (Owen *et al.* 1986). Numbers of Dark-bellied Brent Geese at The Wash and the North Norfolk Coast increased throughout the period 1960-1994, mirroring the rate of change in the population as a whole (Rowcliffe & Mitchell 1998). Since then, the rate of increase has slowed with numbers stabilising in recent winters.

Much feeding on the Wash and North Norfolk Coast is on the extensive saltmarshes, although *Zostera* and *Enteromorpha* are important intertidal foods. Studies undertaken in the 1950s around Scolt Head, North Norfolk, describe birds feeding intertidally through until February on *Zostera* and *Enteromorpha* before moving onto saltmarsh in late February and early March (Ranwell & Downing 1959). As with other sites within the species core range, field feeding has now become a regular occurrence with a large proportion of time in mid winter spent as much as 10 km inland (Summers & Critchley 1990).

2.1.3.3   Internationally important sites

i) The Wash

Five-year mean 95/96-99/2000: 22,874

Site conservation status
SPA (Gibraltar Point: non-qualifying species, The Wash: selection stage 1.2)
Ramsar (The Wash, Gibraltar Point)
NNR (The Wash, Gibraltar Point)
SSSI (The Wash)
IBA (The Wash: criteria A4i, B1i & C3)

Site description and habitat
The embayment's 25,542 ha of intertidal flats (TF5540) is predominantly sand, particularly the outer banks. Fringing these are saltmarshes seaward of the seawalls, which stretch from Snettisham on the east shore around to Gibraltar Point. A saltmarsh restoration programme is in progress along the west coast with purposeful breaching of the sea. The eastern shore from to Heacham to Hunstanton is open with low cliffs, sand dunes then extending to Holme. Behind a shingle barrier running from Snettisham to Heacham are two saline lagoons.

Numbers and trends
Most Dark-bellied Brent Geese arrive at The Wash during October, numbers having stabilised by November with a peak of up to 28,000 birds (Fig. 10 and 11). Numbers remain high into May, with up to 10,000 birds present. The only other British sites that act as spring staging areas for pre-migratory fattening are located in Kent. This is a relatively recent phenomenon, and may thus be related to the increase in the overall population, as traditional spring staging areas become overcrowded (Ebbinge 1992).

Site use
The Wash population's growth has not altered the species focus upon the southwestern coast around Kirton where the saltmarshes are extensively grazed.

ii) North Norfolk Coast

Five-year mean 95/96-99/2000: 10,812

Site conservation status
SPA (North Norfolk Coast: selection stage 1.2)
Ramsar (North Norfolk Coast)
SSSI (North Norfolk Coast)
NNR (various)
IBA (North Norfolk coast: criteria A4i, B1i & C3)

Site description and habitat
From Holme east to Saltholme, the North Norfolk Coast (TF8546) provides an almost 40 km continuous strip of prime waterbird habitat of over 5,900ha. Much of the extensive intertidal sand and mudflats, and some of Europe's best saltmarshes are sheltered by the offshore barrier island of Scolt Head and shingle spit of Blakeney Point. Both of the latter sand dune capped features are actively accreting westwards. From west to east, the intertidal flats change from predominately sand to that of mud, the latter supporting *Zostera* beds. Lagoons of man-made and natural origins, and well-developed sand dunes occur at various locations along the coast.

Numbers and trends
Flocks of Dark-bellied Brent Geese along this coast are best regarded as one group given their movement between harbours. Most arrive during October, increasing in number to between 7,000 and 9,000 birds in February (Fig. 12 and 13). Midwinter peaks as high as 13,000 to 15,000 birds have been recorded. Over 50% of peak numbers remain into March, with most birds leaving for spring staging areas by April.

Site use
Studies in the 1980s identified the temporal use of various habitats the vicinity of Scolts Head, Titchwell to Holkham (Summers & Critchley 1990). In late autumn, birds were found to be feeding on the intertidal flats and in the low-water channels, grazing *Enteromorpha*, *Ulva* and *Zostera*, and on saltmarshes, the latter used particularly at high tide. By late October/early November. they had started to feed on agricultural land inland of the sea wall, usually on wheat fields in early winter and later on grass. By mid March, a high percentage of these birds returned to the intertidal habitats, and saltmarshes in particular were used for the rest of the spring, both at high and low tide.

Summers & Critchley (1990) established that birds moved onto fields sometime after dawn, the timing dependent upon the tide, birds first feeding on the saltmarsh. Departure from field feeding was usually by mass flighting shortly before dusk. The geese were found to roost nocturnally in Norton Creek either on the water high tide or the mudflat and shallow waters of the creeks at low tide. There is no reason to suppose that the temporal usage of habitats by Dark-bellied Brent Geese in the Scolt's Head area has altered significantly since the 1980s.

More recently, the 1997/98 WeBS Low Tide Counts found birds to be spread widely along the coast with a clear preference for saltmarsh away from the sea (Cranswick *et al.* 1999). Densities were highest in Blakeney Harbour and north of Burnham Overy Staithe.

2.1.3.4 Key references

Ranwell & Downing (1959), Summers & Critchley (1990).

2.1.4 Suffolk & Essex

2.1.4.1 Background

The coastal plain of Essex and southeast Suffolk is one of largely intensive arable agricultural broken up by a succession of broad estuaries. These estuaries are typical of a coastal plain form with the exception of Hamford Water (embayment) and Dengie Flats (linear shore). Agriculture has played a significant role in shaping the present estuaries. Sea walls or embankments now protect the majority of the open coast and estuarine shoreline, with land gained at the expense of intertidal flats and marshes. The Blackwater, the largest estuarine complex of this coast, is not alone in losing much of its saltmarsh to agricultural land claim long ago. Now saltmarsh erosion from natural causes is a major issue, with saltmarshes from the Orwell to Stour haven shown substantial erosion, averaging a 20% loss of the original area between 1973 and 1988 (Burd 1992). The erosion of saltmarsh has continued from 1989 to 1998 albeit at different rates than during the previous 15 years (Environment Agency, C.Gibson *in litt.*). For example, erosion rates in the Stour Estuary appeared to be slower between 1988 and 1998 than between1973 and 1988, conversely they were higher in Hamford Water during the latter period. The Environment Agency's study concluded Essex is losing some 40 ha of saltmarsh to erosion each year, 1% of the original area in 1973.

Adjacent to some estuaries, e.g. the Orwell and Colne, are areas of urbanisation and industry with populations of more than 100,000 people. At other estuaries, rather fewer people live adjacent to key sites, with fewer than 5,000 people at Hamford Water and Dengie Flats. The development of urban and industrial areas has, however, been severely hindered by the difficulty of bridging the numerous tidal waters and wetlands. As a consequence, the coast is comparatively unspoilt and includes protected stretches of virtual wilderness. However, major losses of intertidal land to port/commercial development have taken place, in particular at Fagbury Flats (Orwell Estuary) and Bathside Bay (Stour Estuary).

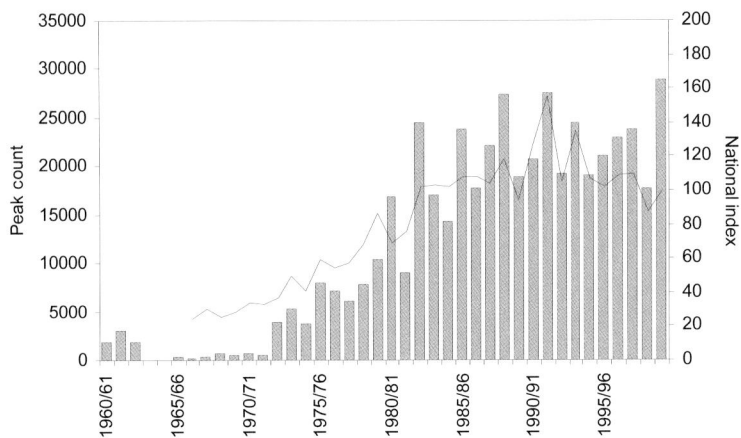

Figure 10. Dark-bellied Brent Geese at The Wash, 1960/61-1999/2000: peak counts (bars) and British index (line) (circles denote years with no known data)

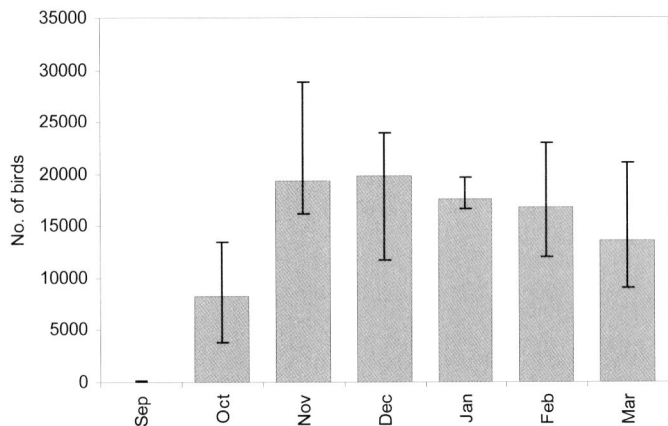

Figure 11. Dark-bellied Brent Geese at The Wash, 1995/96-1999/2000: mean peak counts by month (error bars denote minimum and maximum peak counts during the period)

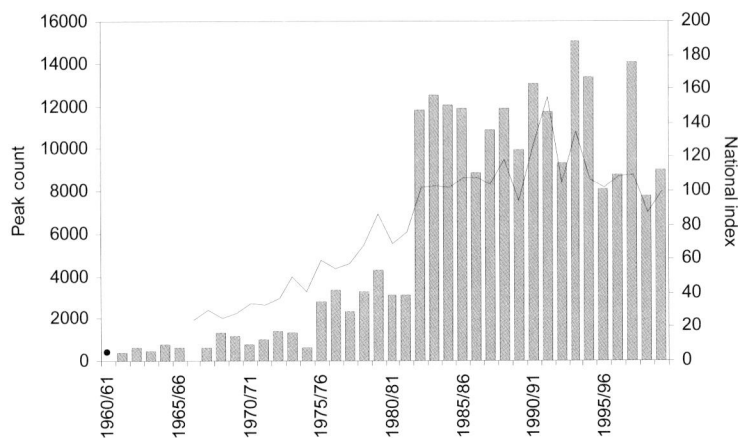

Figure 12. Dark-bellied Brent Geese at the North Norfolk Coast, 1960/61-1999/2000: peak counts (bars) and British index (line) (circles denote years with no known data)

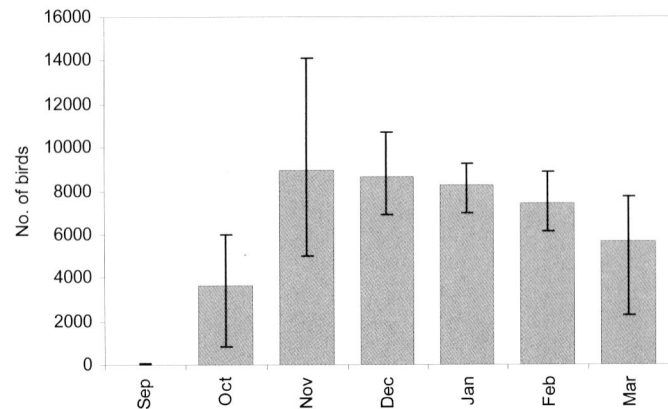

Figure 13. Dark-bellied Brent Geese at the North Norfolk Coast, 1995/96-1999/2000: mean peak counts by month (error bars denote minimum and maximum peak counts during the period)

2.1.4.2   Historical status

Though the literature available provides little information on numbers, the evidence suggests that in the late 1880s Dark-bellied Brent Geese were in some winters very abundant in Suffolk and in others quite scarce (Payn 1978). In Essex at around 1860, 32 punt gunners firing simultaneously shot at least 704 birds at Dengie Flats (Glegg 1929). By the early 1900s, numbers were declining in the region, as globally, and continued to do so until the 1950s. This trend had reversed across the region during the period 1962/63 to 1995/96 and at an overall rate either comparable or below that of the increase witnessed globally (Rowcliffe & Mitchell 1998). Numbers at key sites did not increase in unison. This is exactly as would be expected if birds exhibit a preference for occupancy of key habitats (Moser 1988). More recently for all sites along the Essex/Suffolk coast, numbers appear to have reached equilibrium. In fact there is even the suggestion that numbers may be declining at some sites e.g. the Colne Estuary, reflecting by the national trend (Gregory et al. 2002b).

In a severe winter shortly before the Second World War, Dark-bellied Brent Geese came in at night to feed by moonlight on the tops of Brassicas protruding above the snow at Canewdon on the Crouch Estuary (D. Wood pers. comm.). Additional observations in the mid 1950s indicated that up to 500 birds fed inland on the north Dengie on very high tides with rough seas (D. Wood pers. comm.). It was again in Essex, during the severe winter of 1962/63, that Dark-bellied Brent Geese were first observed feeding on farmland inland of the sea walls in any large numbers in the UK, about 1,000 birds in that winter (St Joseph 1979b). Over 3,000 birds were subsequently found foraging inside the sea walls during the winter of 1969/70. It was only then that foraging inland of the sea walls on farmland became a regular and widespread behaviour. By winter 1975/76, up to 75% of the total number of birds spending the winter in Essex/Suffolk would be foraging inland at a given time (Owen et al. 1986). This behaviour remains equally as prevalent along this coast today, the intensity greatest in mid winter.

The region's coast, together with the adjacent reservoirs, comprise one of the most important complexes of habitat for waterbirds in Northwest Europe, including over 10% of the world population of Dark-bellied Brent Geese. Though Dark-bellied Brent Geese move between sites in the region, each are important in their own right. The highest numbers of Dark-bellied Brent Geese in the region are present from November through to March, with occupancy by substantial numbers through to April at some sites. Prior to December, studies of marked birds at Foulness have shown that some of the birds using the Essex/Suffolk coast initially take up residency on the Thames Estuary from October, prior to the depletion of *Zostera* stocks (St Joseph 1979a).

2.1.4.3   Internationally important sites

i) Hamford Water

Five-year mean 95/96-99/2000: 6,829

Site conservation status
SPA (Hamford Water: selection stage 1.2)
Ramsar (Hamford Water)
NNR (Hamford Water)
SSSI (Hamford Water)
IBA (Hamford Water: criteria A4i, B1i & C3)

Site description and habitat
Hamford Water (TM2225) is a large, shallow estuarine basin whose mouth is bordered by two shingle spits topped by sand dunes and shell bank. Within is a mosaic of islands, tidal creeks, mudflats, sandflats and saltmarshes, the latter lying mainly outside the sea walls and on the islands, or within breached sea walls. Towards the sea, soft intertidal mudflats support beds of *Enteromorpha* and now very little *Zostera* remains.

Numbers and trends
Much variability exists in the timing and extent of winter peak counts, this perhaps a reflection of the interchange that occurs between Hamford Water and estuaries to the north and Holland Haven reserve to the south. In general, however, an early winter peak occurs in November/December ranging from 2,300, following a poor breeding season, to 9,300 birds (Fig. 14 and 15). Numbers often remain high through into February, and often March. An exception was in winter 1995/96 when a comparatively stable wintering population of 3,000-4,000 birds leapt to 14,000 following an influx in March. On 7 March 1996, 75% of the rings read at Wade track cereal fields were on birds not seen in this country before whilst the other 25% were regular visitors to Hamford Water (D. Wood pers. comm.). The weather on the continent was unseasonably cold at that time and probably forced birds to cross the North Sea from the Continent.

Site use
Field feeding Dark-bellied Brent Geese particularly favour Horsey Island, one of the first locations where this habit became established in Britain. By 1979, birds in the south of Hamford Water were already spending about 87% of their daily feeding

time on inland feeding areas in late winter, whilst a minority fed exclusively on saltmarsh (White-Robinson 1982). However, there has been a notable reduction in the numbers of birds feeding inland in the vicinity of Hamford Water in recent years (D. Wood pers. comm.).

ii) Colne Estuary

Five-year mean 95/96-99/2000: 3,762

Site conservation status
SPA (Colne Estuary [Mid-Essex Coast Phase 2]: selection stage 1.2)
Ramsar (Colne Estuary [Mid-Essex Coast Phase 2])
NNR (Colne Estuary)
SSSI (Colne Estuary)
IBA (Mid-Essex coast: criteria A4i, B1i & C3)

Site description and habitat
The Colne Estuary (TM0614) consists of numerous channels, and supports extensive areas of intertidal flats and saltmarsh. Within the inner estuary, the intertidal flats are composed largely of mud, changing to a mixture of sand and mud on the outer reaches. Flanking the estuary is agriculture, grazing marshes and localised areas of light industry, small ports and towns, such as Brightlingsea.

Numbers and trends
Between 2,500 and 4,300 birds have been recorded within the period November to January, numbers fluctuating during the winter by a factor of up to 50% (Fig. 16 and 17). During the late 1980s and early 1990s, numbers were typically much higher, peaking at around 5,000-7,000 birds. By March, 1,000–2,000 birds typically remain on site.

iii) Blackwater Estuary

Five-year mean 95/96-99/2000: 8,891

Site conservation status
SPA (Blackwater Estuary [Mid-Essex Coast Phase 4]: selection stage 1.2)
Ramsar (Blackwater Estuary [Mid-Essex Coast Phase 4])
NNR (Blackwater Estuary)
SSSI (Blackwater Estuary)
IBA (Mid-Essex coast: criteria A4i, B1i & C3)

Site description and habitat
The Blackwater Estuary (TL9307) is a diverse mosaic of river channels, creeks, intertidal flats, saltmarshes and two islands. Though a third of the estuary's intertidal zone remains saltmarsh, extensive land-claim has left only pockets of this previously extensive habitat within the more sheltered parts. Particularly within the bays and creeks, a large

proportion of the intertidal area is mudflat. Elsewhere, some intertidal areas are characterised by shingle and shell banks, and gravel beds. *Enteromorpha* coverage is extensive on the upper reaches of the estuary. A reversal of the land claim of saltmarsh through managed retreat is now underway in parts of the Blackwater.

Numbers and trends
Numbers peak during the period November to January, generally between 8,500 and 11,000 birds (Fig. 18 and 19). In some years, the birds using Old Hall Marshes and Tollesbury Wick have not been included in WeBS counts, as in 1998 when the peak count for the whole site was low. Typically, numbers remain high into March. In the 1980s, birds foraged up to 2.5 miles inland, these birds usually being missed by WeBS. With their inclusion, site counts in January were never much under 12,000 birds and at times up to 14,500 (D. Wood pers. comm.).

Site use
In early winter most Dark-bellied Brent Geese forage out on the estuary mudflats (Gibbs 1993). From late November onwards, flocks switch to foraging on farmland, the estuary becoming principally a site of refuge, when birds are disturbed from inland, and probably for roosting at night. In the 1980s, birds foraged up to 2.5 miles inland (D. Wood pers. comm.). Largest numbers occur on fields at Old Hall Marshes (improved pasture), North Blackwater (mainly between Joyce's Farm and Rolls Farm), Osea Island (set-a-side), the Northey Island area and the Steeple and Mayland area (D. Wood pers. comm., Gibbs 1993). In recent winters, up to 2,500 birds have been recorded at Old Hall Marshes/Tollesbury and no more than 2,000 at Steeple/Mayland (D. Wood pers. comm.). The latter site has supported up to 7,000 birds in the past.

Figure 14. Dark-bellied Brent Geese at Hamford Water, 1960/61-1999/2000: peak counts (bars) and British index (line) (circles denote years with no known data)

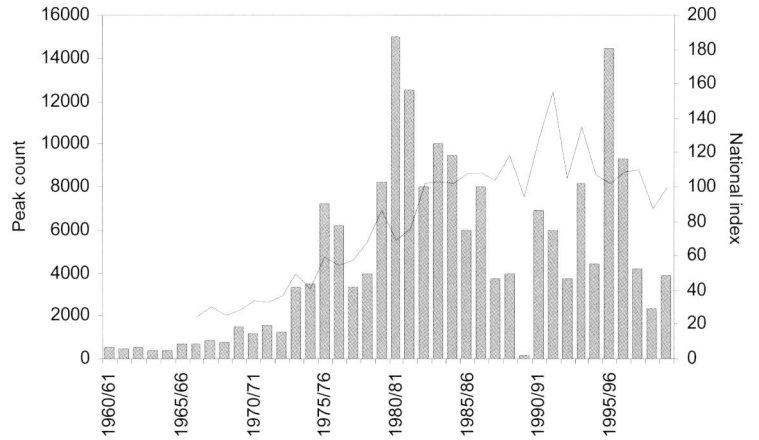

Figure 15. Dark-bellied Brent Geese at Hamford Water, 1995/96-1999/2000: mean peak counts by month (error bars denote minimum and maximum peak counts during the period)

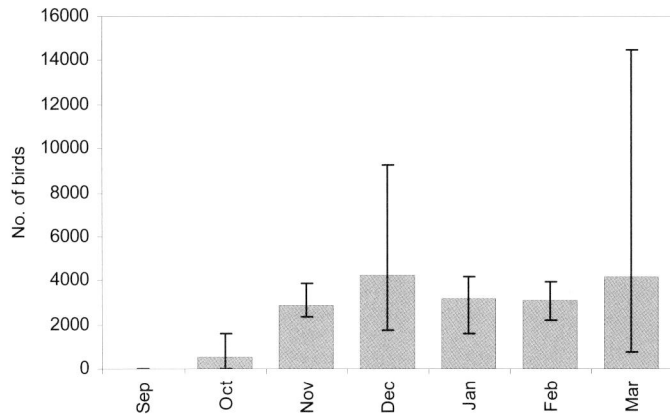

Figure 16. Dark-bellied Brent Geese at the Colne Estuary, 1960/61-1999/2000: peak counts (bars) and British index (line) (circles denote years with no known data)

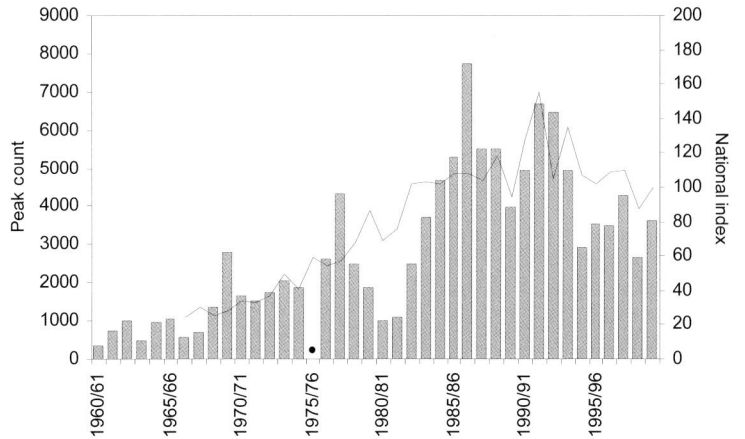

Figure 17. Dark-bellied Brent Geese at the Colne Estuary, 1995/96-1999/2000: mean peak counts by month (error bars denote minimum and maximum peak counts during the period)

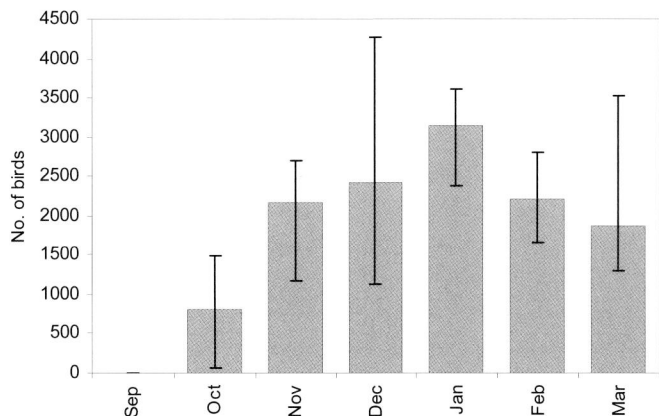

iv) Crouch-Roach Estuary

Five-year mean 95/96-99/2000: 4,539

Site conservation status:
SPA (Crouch and Roach Estuaries [Mid-Essex coast phase 3]: selection stage 1.2)
Ramsar (Crouch and Roach Estuaries [Mid-Essex coast phase 3])
SSSI (Crouch and Roach Estuaries)
IBA (Mid-Essex coast: criteria A4i, B1i & C3)

Site description and habitat
Following the loss of most intertidal flats by land-claim to agriculture, this habitat is limited to narrow mudflats in the Crouch and creeks of the Roach (TQ8496). Likewise, extensive areas of saltmarsh are now confined to Fambridge and Bridgemarsh Island, mid estuary on the Crouch. Elsewhere, small pockets of saltmarsh exist in the bays along the Crouch, flanking its upper reaches, and within the creeks of the Roach. Habitat management includes creation of high-level mudflats, a brackish lagoon, and restoration of saltmarsh, as well as management of grazing marsh for Dark-bellied Brent Geese. Much of the site is flanked by sea walls and embankments behind which is an agricultural landscape with some urbanisation.

Numbers and trends
A few birds arrive on site by October, the main arrival being during November onwards, peaking typically in January at 5,000-6,000 birds or lower following a poor breeding season (Fig. 20 and 21). Though not necessarily reflected by the whole estuary counts, in recent years no fewer than 3,000 birds have regularly been counted on site before late March (D. Wood pers. comm.). Unusually high counts in the early 1990s and 1984/85 coincided with use of the estuary by all three, generally discrete, local flocks (D. Wood pers. comm.; see below). The low peak count in 1998 was an artefact of topographical counting difficulties rather than a temporary fall in numbers (D. Wood pers. comm.). In recent years, numbers in this area are considered to have fallen rather less than in other parts of Essex (D. Wood pers. comm.).

Site use
At low tide, the majority of birds are found foraging inland on fields. The remaining birds have been recorded at Brandy Hole Creek, the west end of Bridgemarsh Island, and at the confluence of the Crouch and Roach rivers (Cranswick *et al.* 1997).

The Crouch-Roach Estuary is used by three, generally discrete, flocks of Dark-bellied Brent Geese (D. Wood pers. comm.). The upper Crouch flock feeds mainly west of Bridgemarsh Island where it roosts. The flock roosting at Ray Sands on South Dengie feeds inland on south Dengie, the north side of the lower Crouch, the north side of Foulness and Wallasea Island (see Dengie Flats). The third flock, roosting on Thames side, feeds mainly at south Foulness, Potton Island, Wakering and the Roach at times. This detailed knowledge of site usage is the result of an extensive colour-ringing and ring-reading programme undertaken by Andrew St Joseph.

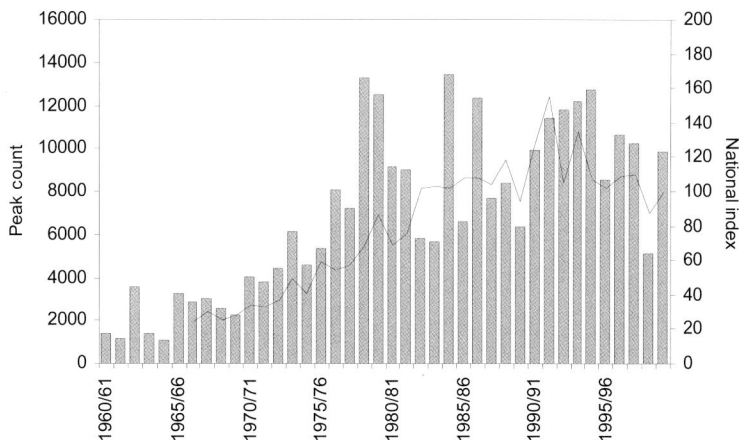

Figure. 18. Dark-bellied Brent Geese at the Blackwater Estuary, 1960/61-1999/2000: peak counts (bars) and British index (line) (circles denote years with no known data)

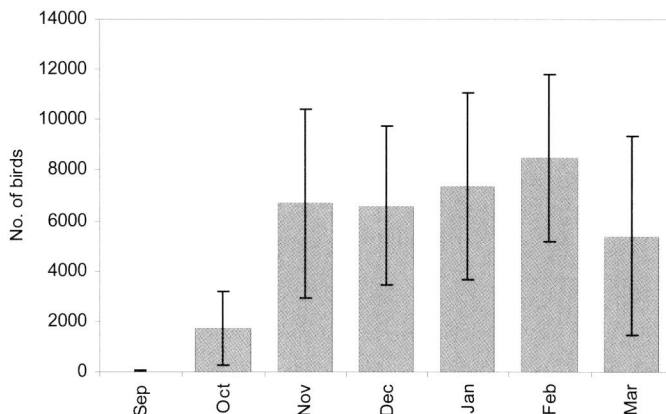

Figure. 19. Dark-bellied Brent Geese at the Blackwater Estuary, 1995/96-1999/2000: mean peak counts by month (error bars denote minimum and maximum peak counts during the period)

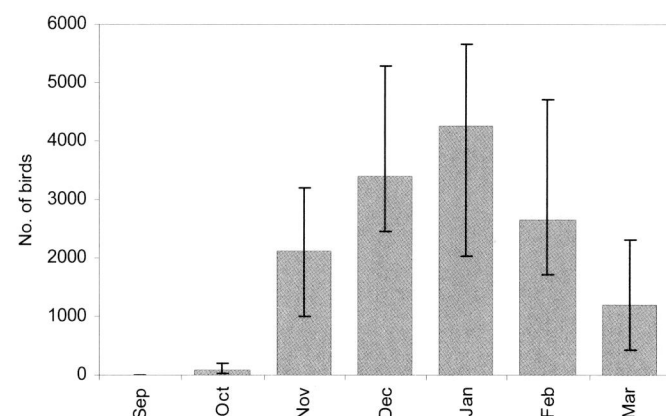

Figure. 20. Dark-bellied Brent Geese at the Crouch-Roach Estuary, 1960/61-1999/2000: peak counts (bars) and British index (line) (circles denote years with no known data)

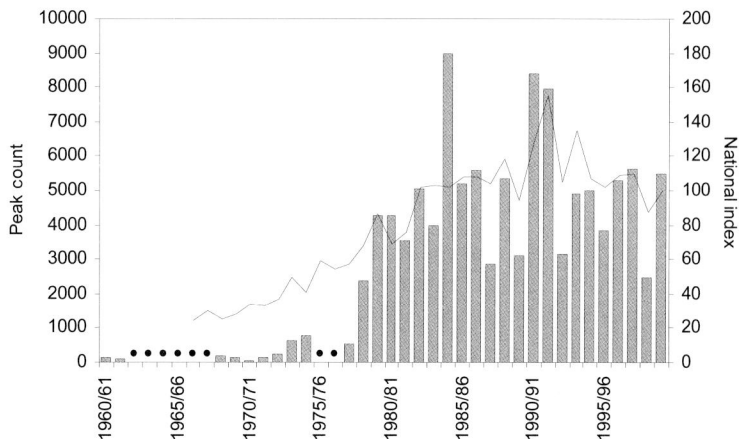

Figure. 21. Dark-bellied Brent Geese at the Crouch-Roach Estuary, 1995/96-1999/2000: mean peak counts by month (error bars denote minimum and maximum peak counts during the period)

2.1.4.4 Nationally important sites

i) Deben Estuary

Five-year mean 95/96-99/2000: 2,269

Site conservation status
SPA (Deben Estuary: non-qualifying species)
Ramsar (Deben Estuary)
SSSI (Deben Estuary)
IBA (Deben Estuary: non-listed species)

Site description and habitat
The Deben is a narrow estuary (TM2942) extending southeastwards from Woodbridge for a distance of over 12 km, reaching the sea just to the north of Felixstowe. Intertidal mudflats are extensive within the estuary's inner reaches but more restricted downstream to the mouth. Extensive saltmarsh exists on both banks throughout the estuary. Away from the town of Woodbridge, agriculture largely surrounds the estuary.

Numbers and trends
No more than 10% of peak numbers have arrived by October, with the main arrival period extending through to December (Fig. 22 and 23). Peak counts frequently coincide with an apparent small influx in January or February, with numbers reaching 2,000 to 3,300 birds. When there is no influx, the peak has occurred earlier in December, although never exceeding 2,200 birds. With the occasional exception, few birds remain through into March.

Site use
A WeBS Low Tide Count in 1998/9 found foraging birds concentrated at Sutton Flats and the flats from Ramsholt downstream (Pollitt *et al.* 2000). Birds also forage inland on agricultural land (D. Wood pers. comm.). Field reading of colour-ringed Dark-bellied Brent Geese suggests some interchange of birds between the Deben and Orwell Estuaries (D. Wood pers. comm.).

ii) Orwell Estuary

Five-year mean 95/96-99/2000: 1,219

Site conservation status
SPA (Stour and Orwell Estuaries: selection stage 1.3)
Ramsar (Stour and Orwell Estuaries)
SSSI (Orwell Estuary)
IBA (Stour and Orwell Estuaries: non-listed species)

Site description and habitat
The Orwell Estuary (TM2238) is long and narrow and supports extensive mudflats on the upper reaches, these flats become increasingly sandy towards the estuary mouth. Amongst the estuary's tributaries and embayments are patches of saltmarsh, none large in area. The upper reaches are enclosed by Ipswich, the mid estuary flanked by farmland and wet meadows after which the port of Felixstowe on the north bank dominates the lower reaches.

Numbers and trends
The pattern of winter occurrence is variable. Numbers frequently peak at 700-1,300 birds in February after a protracted arrival period (Fig. 24 and 25). However, in some recent winters, the peak has occurred earlier in December or January following the arrival of a higher proportion of peak numbers by October. Unlike other sites, this difference in phenology appears not to be related to breeding success.

Site use
The majority of birds concentrate at low tide at the southern end of the estuary, occurring only in small numbers further north, with Shotley Marshes, Jill's Hole and Trimley Marshes being favoured in particular (Cranswick *et al.* 1997, Waters *et al.* 1998, Pollitt *et al.* 2000). Reading of colour-ringed Dark-bellied Brent Geese in fields suggests there is no or little interchange of birds between the Orwell Estuary and adjacent Stour Estuary (D. Wood pers. comm.).

iii) Stour Estuary

Five-year mean 95/96-99/2000: 1,973

Site conservation status
SPA (Stour and Orwell Estuaries: selection stage 1.3)
Ramsar (Stour and Orwell Estuaries)
SSSI (Stour Estuary)
IBA (Stour and Orwell Estuary: non-listed species)

Site description and habitat
The Stour Estuary (TM1732) is long, with an indented shoreline that has five main bays. Much of the extensive mudflats are within the bays, with those intertidal flats close to the estuary's confluence with the Orwell becoming sandy. The intertidal flats of Erwarton and Holbrook Bays previously supported extensive beds of *Zostera* that may no longer be present (C. Gibson pers. comm.). Steep shoreline topography prohibits more than a fringe of saltmarsh around the estuary with the exception of Erwarton and Copperas Bays where expansive marshes exist. *Spartina* forms more than 25% of the saltmarsh area.

Figure 22. Dark-bellied Brent Geese at the Deben Estuary, 1960/61-1999/2000: peak counts (bars) and British index (line) (circles denote years with no known data)

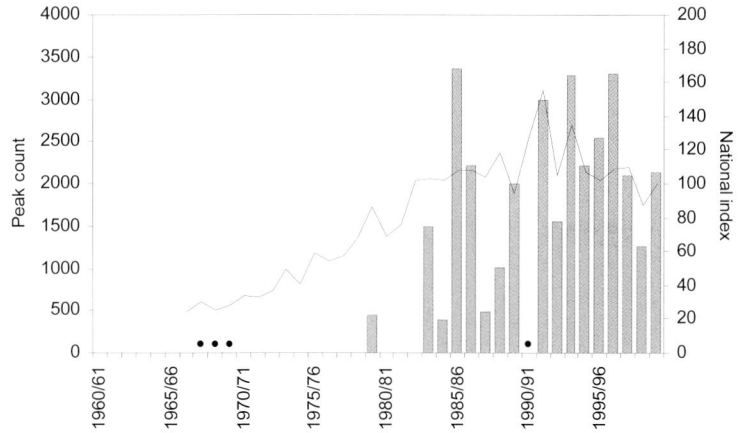

Figure 23. Dark-bellied Brent Geese at the Deben Estuary, 1995/96-1999/2000: mean peak counts by month (error bars denote minimum and maximum peak counts during the period)

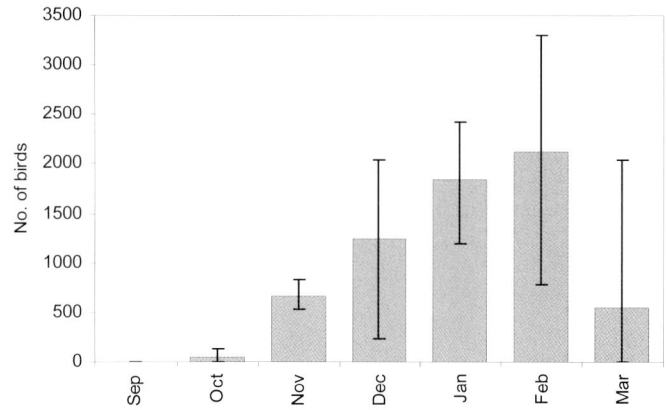

Figure 24. Dark-bellied Brent Geese at the Orwell Estuary, 1960/61-1999/2000: peak counts (bars) and British index (line) (circles denote years with no known data)

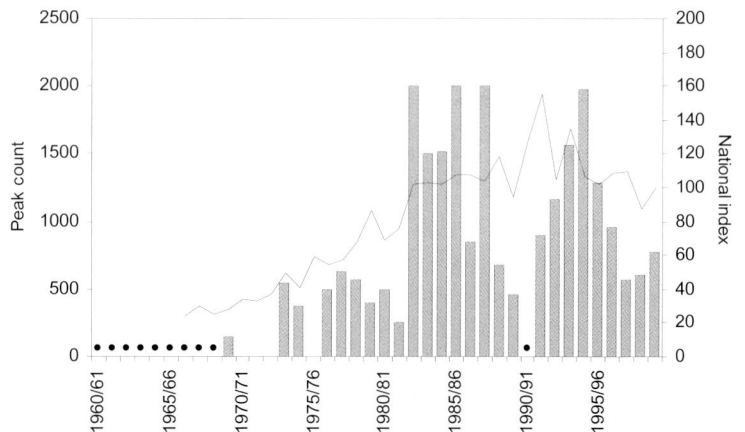

Figure 25. Dark-bellied Brent Geese at the Orwell Estuary, 1995/96-1999/2000: mean peak counts by month (error bars denote minimum and maximum peak counts during the period)

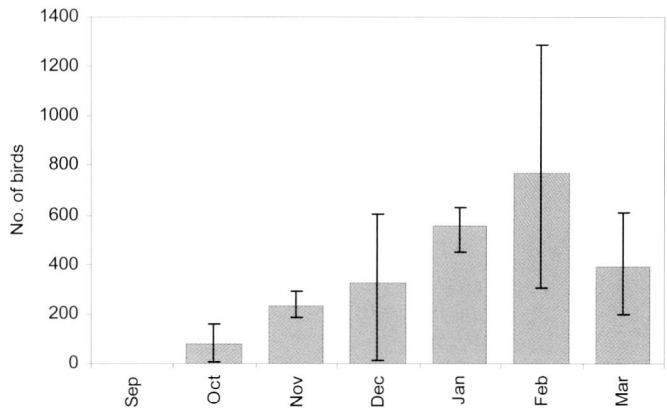

Numbers and trends
Numbers typically peak in December, and then again in March with the maximum numbers attained being 1,700 to 2,400 birds (Fig. 26 and 27). In recent years, numbers in October have frequently exceeded 50% of winter peaks. Furthermore, prolonged spring staging is now occurring at the site, with over 500 birds present until late May (D. Wood pers. comm.).

Site use
Dark-bellied brent Geese are dispersed widely across the estuary at low tide (Waters *et al.* 1998). Reading of colour-ringed Dark-bellied Brent Geese in fields suggests there is little or no interchange of birds between the Orwell Estuary and adjacent Stour Estuary (D. Wood pers. comm.).

iv) Dengie Flats
Five-year mean 95/96-99/2000: 2,176

Site conservation status
SPA (Dengie [Mid-Essex coast phase 1]: selection stage 1.3)
Ramsar (Dengie [Mid-Essex coast phase 1])
NNR (Dengie)
SSSI (Dengie)
IBA (Mid-Essex coast: criteria A4i, B1i & C3)

Site description and habitat
Dengie Flats (TM0300) is one continuous intertidal mudflat backed by saltmarsh that stretches almost eight miles along the open coast between the Blackwater and Crouch-Roach estuaries. In the transition between the two habitats is a zone of mud-mounds with shell-lined gullies. Extensive patches of *Enteromorpha* are distributed across the intertidal flats. Inland of the seawall is largely an agricultural landscape amongst which marshes remain at Sandbeach Meadows and Bridgewick Marshes, only the former is grazed (D. Wood pers. comm.*).* Managed creation of saltmarsh is being undertaken south of the main saltmarsh on Ray Sands.

Numbers and trends
Counts would suggest that the pattern of usage of this site is highly variable, both within and between winters. The peak winter count in recent years has ranged from 1,500 to 2,600 and has occurred at various times between November and March (Fig. 28 and 29). Numbers vary markedly between October and March, suggesting some interchange between this and adjacent sites. Numbers roosting on the Ray Sand are often higher than daytime counts because birds move between different sites in the area (D. Wood pers. comm.; see below).

Site use
As mentioned above, the south Dengie flock that roosts on Ray Sand, feeds inland at South Dengie, the north side of the lower Crouch, the north side of Foulness and on Wallasea Island (D. Wood pers. comm.). The north Dengie flock is completely separate, occasionally numbering 700 birds, with those birds colour-ringed in this flock having not been seen elsewhere in Essex. Occasionally, birds from Old Hall Marshes on the Blackwater Estuary join the flock. As well as feeding inland, many birds at Dengie Flats feed on the saltmarsh for 3-4 hours around high tide. In the past, Dark-bellied Brent Geese foraged on the grazed marshes at Sandbeach Meadows.

2.1.4.5 Key references

Glegg (1929), Payn (1978), St Joseph (1979b).

2.1.5 Thames & North Kent

2.1.5.1 Background

Being adjacent to London, the largest conurbation in Britain, significantly influences the outer Thames Estuary. Oil refineries and associated petrochemical industries, power stations, docks and industrial estates dominate the outer estuary's north bank east to the conurbation of Southend-on-Sea. Such urban and industrial growth has been at the expense of large-scale land claim of the coastal marshes and intertidal flats e.g. Canvey Island, and opposite Southend-on-Sea, the Isle of Grain. In contrast, the south shore west of the Isle of Grain is dominated by extensive enclosed grazing marshes and arable land, stretching 23 km east to Gravesend, with limited industrial development. Within this much altered landscape, Dark-bellied Brent Geese can be found using any suitable intertidal area, even that adjacent to the major industrial developments.

In marked contrast to the remainder of the north shore, east of Shoeburyness, is the wilderness of Foulness Island and Maplin Sands, the largest continuous area of intertidal flats in Britain (over 11,500 ha). The lack of development of this coast is a consequence of the ownership and use of the majority as a firing range by the Ministry of Defence with access strictly controlled.

Figure 26. Dark-bellied Brent Geese at the
Stour Estuary, 1960/61-1999/2000:
peak counts (bars) and British
index (line) (circles denote years
with no known data)

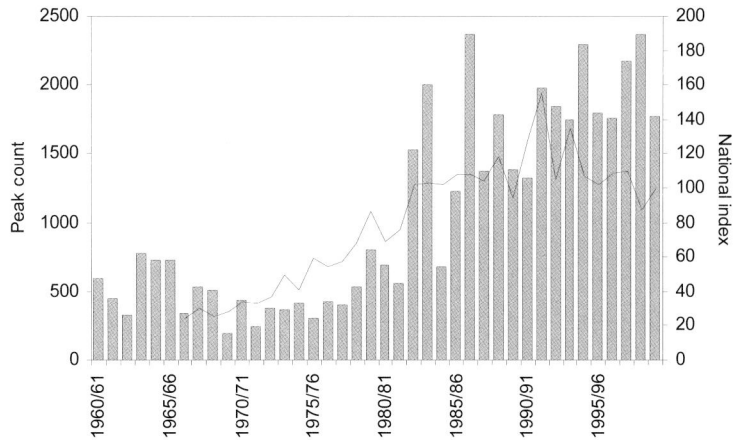

Figure 27. Dark-bellied Brent Geese at the
Stour Estuary, 1995/96-1999/2000:
mean peak counts by month (error
bars denote minimum and
maximum peak counts during the
period)

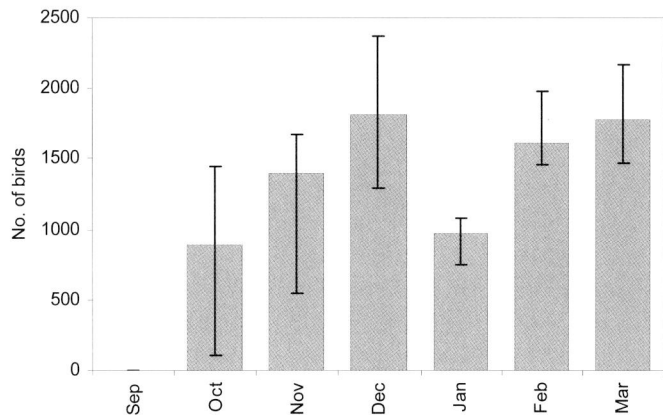

Figure 28. Dark-bellied Brent Geese at Dengie
Flats, 1960/61-1999/2000: peak
counts (bars) and British index
(line) (circles denote years with no
known data)

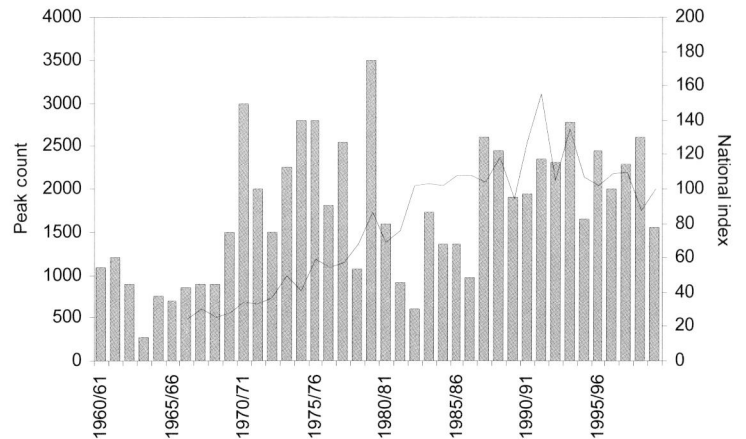

Figure 29. Dark-bellied Brent Geese at Dengie
Flats, 1995/96-1999/2000: mean
peak counts by month (error bars
denote minimum and maximum
peak counts during the period)

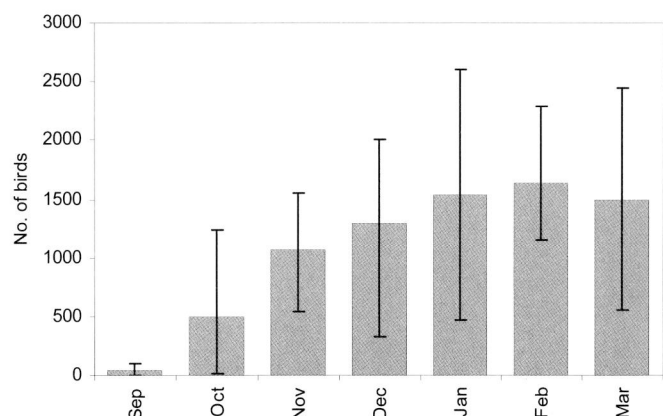

South of the Thames, the rolling North Downs closely borders the coast with the two eventually merging in the east on the Thanet coast. The North Kent coast from Thanet west to the Isle of Grain is one of contrast with stretches of cliff, rocky shoreline, sand and mud beaches interspersed with rock, and intertidal areas of mudflats and saltmarsh. Centred upon this coast is the Isle of Sheppey within the confluences of the Swale and Medway with the Thames. The agriculture flanking this coast is mostly arable, with some pasture containing pockets of enclosed grazing marsh. The landscape is further composed of a network of urban and industrial centres from which the populous, in common with the rest of the region, increasingly seeks recreational pursuits within the Thames Estuary.

2.1.5.2   Historical status

In the late 19th century, the Dark-bellied Brent Goose was described as a regular visitor to the Thames, Swale and Medway Estuaries in Kent, with 'immense' numbers recorded during severe winters when birds would also be recorded in small numbers elsewhere along the coast (Gillham & Homes 1950). There is no reason to expect that the species was not also a regular winter visitor to the northern shore of the outer Thames Estuary though firm evidence is lacking. Numbers thereafter probably declined as described for elsewhere in Britain. Indeed during the 1930s and 1940s, Gillham & Homes (1950) quote wintering numbers rarely exceeding 50, 20 and 100 birds on the Thames Marshes (Cliffe to Medway), Medway Estuary and Swale Estuary, respectively. In severe winters, however, influxes of up to 300 birds have been recorded at these sites.

From the low point in the global population of Dark-bellied Brent Geese in the 1950s, the Thames Estuary was one of several nuclei from where numbers in Britain increased. Indeed, Rowcliffe and Mitchell's (1998) analysis of the period 1960 – 1996 suggests that carrying capacity for the 'Foulness and the inner Thames Estuary' had been attained by the 1960s. This is not evident from inspection of the peak winter counts for the Thames Estuary which suggest stability occurred much later in the early 1980s (Fig. 31). This discrepancy arises because, in contrast to elsewhere in Britain, numbers of Dark-bellied Brent Geese at the latter site typically peak during October or November; Rowcliffe and Mitchell (1998) presented counts from January alone. Rowcliffe and Mitchell's (1998) analysis also suggested that when treating flocks from the Medway Estuary and Swale Estuary as one, the sites were below their natural limits for the species.

In the during the 1930s and 1940s, Dark-bellied Brent Geese foraged across the mudflats, saltings, *Spartina* marshes within the Medway Estuary and, only during floods, on freshwater marshes (Gillham & Homes 1950). Now, as elsewhere in adjacent coasts, coastal field feeding has been a regular occurrence since the 1970s, particularly in mid winter.

The flocks of Dark-bellied Brent Geese that use the Foulness area have been studied intensively by Andrew St Joseph and as a consequence of the proposed airport at Maplin Sands (St Joseph 1979a).

2.1.5.3   Internationally important sites

i) Thames Estuary

Five-year mean 95/96-99/2000: 12,913

Site conservation status:
SPA (Foulness [Mid-Essex Coast Phase 5]: selection stage 1.3; Benfleet & Southend Marshes: selection stage 1.2; Thames Estuary and Marshes)
Ramsar (Foulness [Mid-Essex Coast Phase 5], Benfleet & Southend Marshes, Thames Estuary and Marshes: non-qualifying species)
NNR (Leigh)
SSSI (Mucking Flats and Marshes, South Thames Estuary and Marshes)
IBA (Mid-Essex coast: criteria A4i, B1i & C3: Benfleet and Southend Marshes: criteria A4i, B1i & C3; Thames Estuary and Marshes: non-listed species)

Site description and habitat
The open estuarine coast of Foulness is dominated by over 11,500 ha of continuous intertidal flats known as Maplin Sands. It is predominately sandy but with the upper kilometre muddier, the intertidal supporting extensive *Zostera* beds (325 ha). Saltmarsh narrowly fringes the upper shore, this broadening to a large expanse at Foulness Point in the north, which supports one of the largest remaining areas of *Spartina maritima* in Europe. Farmland principally flanks the shoreline.

Continuing west along this northern shore, from Shoeburyness to Coryton , the intertidal flats are of mud with a high sand content. The wide expanse of flats at Leigh supports large beds of *Zostera* and *Enteromorpha*. Though adjacent industry and urban areas dominate much of the shore, patches of saltmarsh do remain, as do grazing marshes enclosed by sea walls on the upper reaches of tributaries at Canvey Island.

On the south bank of the Thames, the estuary (TQ7880) is flanked by the extensive enclosed grazing marshes and arable land of the South Thames Marshes, 3 km at its broadest point. Seaward, the extensive mudflats at Blyth Sands are exposed at low tide. Saltmarsh along the upper shore is largely restricted to the embayments and creeks, Yantlet creek supporting the largest remaining area. The site's eastern most limits are the Isle of Grain and Foulness, on opposite banks.

Numbers and trends
In contrast to elsewhere in Britain, numbers of Dark-bellied Brent Geese at this site typically peak during October or November, at around 10,000 – 17,000 birds, with the majority using Maplin Sands (Fig. 30 and 31). Counts made in winter 1999/2000 missed the October peak (D. Wood pers. comm.). A sharp drop in numbers occurs by December as stocks of their preferred food source, *Zostera*, are depleted, some birds dispersing to the English south coast, France and to other sites along the east coast (St Joseph 1979a). Numbers during the remainder of the winter are quite variable, in some years a second peak occurring late winter, with few birds remaining into April.

Site use
The majority of Dark-bellied Brent Geese at the Thames Estuary use Maplin Sands. Elsewhere, a WeBS Low Tide Count during winter 1999/2000 recorded most birds between Canvey and Two Tree Islands, east to Westcliffe-on-Sea, with smaller numbers between Egypt Bay and Allhallows (Musgrove *et al.* 2001).

2.1.5.4   Nationally important sites

i) Medway Estuary

Five-year mean 95/96-99/2000: 2,482

Site conservation status
SPA (Medway Estuary and Marshes: selection stage 1.2)
Ramsar (Medway Estuary and Marshes)
SSSI (Medway Estuary and Marshes)
IBA (Medway Estuary and Marshes: criteria A4i, B1i & C3)

Site description and habitat
The Medway Estuary (TQ8471) forms a single tidal system with the Swale with which it flanks the Isle of Sheppey on three sides, the north side being the Thames Estuary. Its predominately muddy intertidal flats form the largest such area on the south bank of the outer Thames. Important to Dark-bellied Brent

Geese are the extensive beds of algae and *Zostera* that the mudflats support. Large areas of saltmarsh remain much as isolated islands and areas previously enclosed within sea walls that have since been breached allowing regular inundation by the tide. Behind existing sea walls are enclosed extensive grazing marshes that along with the saltmarshes drained by a complexity of tidal channels.

Numbers and trends
A substantial proportion of peak numbers arrive by October, after which numbers are variable, peaking any time between November and February at 1,800 to 3,000 birds (Fig. 32 and 33). Up to 700 birds remain into May.

Site use
The 1996/97 WeBS Low Tide Counts found Dark-bellied Brent Geese occurring widely across the estuary, with largest numbers concentrated on the south shore (Halstrow and Otterham) and in the north at Colemouth creeks (Waters *et al.* 1998).

ii) Swale Estuary

Five-year mean 95/96-99/2000: 2,172

Site conservation status
SPA (The Swale: selection stage 1.3)
Ramsar (The Swale)
NNR (The Swale)
SSSI (The Swale)
IBA (The Swale: non-listed species)

Site description and habitat
The Swale Estuary (TQ9765) forms a single tidal system with the Medway with which it flanks the Isle of Sheppey on three sides, the north side being the Thames Estuary. The estuary's extensive mudflats become sandy towards the mouth with beds of *Zostera* on the southern shore near Faversham. Saltmarsh is most extensive on the northern shore that includes that sheltering behind the sand/shingle spit of Shellness at the estuary's mouth. Extensive brackish and freshwater grazing-marshes border both shores, these much used by Dark-bellied Brent Geese.

Numbers and trends
The site's phenology is comparable to that observed in the other half of the tidal system, the Medway Estuary, the lack of synchrony in peak counts between sites not necessarily expected if significant interchange occurs (Fig. 34 and 35). A substantial proportion of peak numbers arrives by October after which numbers are variable, the flock size peaking any time between November and March at 1,500 to 3,500 birds. Few birds remain into April.

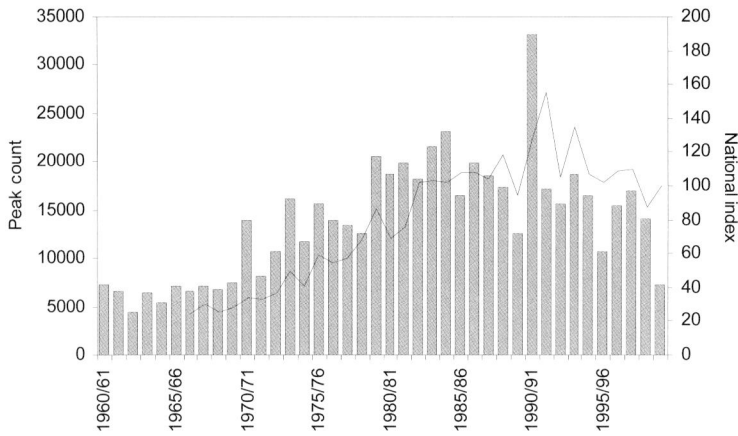

Figure 30. Dark-bellied Brent Geese at the Thames Estuary, 1960/61-1999/2000: peak counts (bars) and British index (line) (circles denote years with no known data)

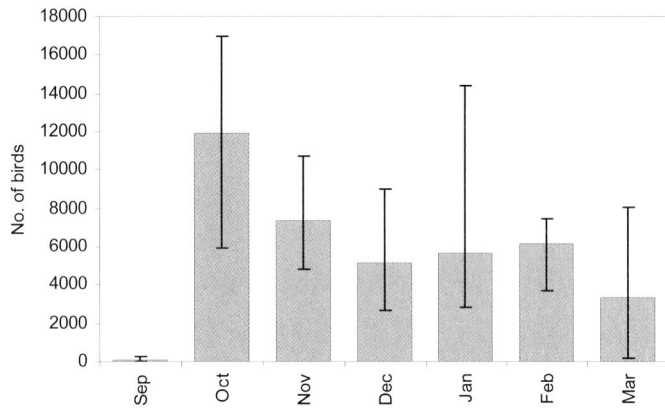

Figure 31. Dark-bellied Brent Geese at the Thames Estuary, 1995/96-1999/2000: mean peak counts by month (error bars denote minimum and maximum peak counts during the period)

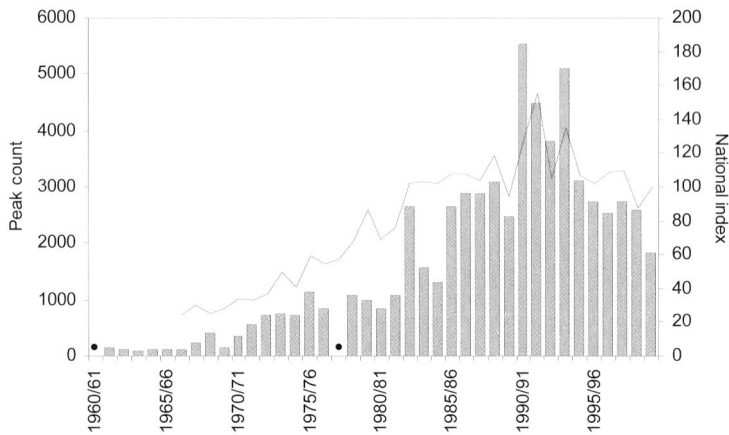

Figure 32. Dark-bellied Brent Geese at the Medway Estuary, 1960/61-1999/2000: peak counts (bars) and British index (line) (circles denote years with no known data)

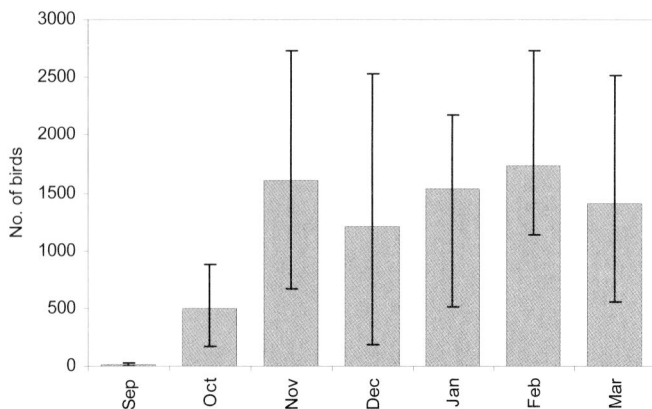

Figure 33. Dark-bellied Brent Geese at the Medway Estuary, 1995/96-1999/2000: mean peak counts by month (error bars denote minimum and maximum peak counts during the period)

Site use

Just outside of the estuary, Dark-bellied Brent Geese often roost on the open sea off the Leysdown-Shellness shore (Owen *et al.* 1986). The brackish and freshwater grazing marshes bordering both estuary shores are much used by Dark-bellied Brent Geese.

2.1.5.5   Other sites

The estuary of the River Stour dominates the section of the Thanet coast covered by the site known as the Thanet Coast (TR2669). Expansive intertidal flats of sand and mud in Pegwell Bay and the adjacent Sandwich Flats to the south form the estuary's mouth. The Stour enters the bay via a 35 km long narrow intertidal channel whose entrance is diverted northwards along the coast by a shingle bar topped inland by sand dunes. Along this channel land claim has largely removed much of the saltmarsh, the exception being the marshes flanking the east bank of the diverted channel. However, saltmarsh has developed within Pegwell Bay at the River Stour's mouth, this being colonised by *Spartina*. Chalk cliffs face the north shore of Pegwell Bay with the town of Ramsgate and its hover-port at the north end.

The pattern of wintering numbers varies little between years unlike the magnitude of the peak count that ranges between 400 and 1,420 birds, typically occurring in January (Fig. 36 and 37). The five-year mean value for 1995/96-1999/2000 was of 781 birds. This site surpassed the national qualifying level in winter 1999/2000.

2.1.5.6   Key references

Gillham & Homes (1950).

2.1.6   West Sussex

2.1.6.1   Background

In West Sussex, an extensive low-lying, flat plain runs between the South Downs and the sea. Much of the coastal plain is agricultural, intensively cultivated, with considerable urban development principally along the coast where it is extensive. In the west, the natural harbours of Pagham and Chichester are the coast's major estuarine habitats, whilst in the east only the small narrow estuaries of the Adur and Arun break the otherwise open coast shoreline of sand and shingle. Agricultural land-claim in the region has seen a major reversal when a breach of the sea walls by the sea enclosing Pagham Harbour as a whole in the 19th century reverted the Bay back to intertidal.

2.1.6.2   Historical status

Prior to the 1940s, Dark-bellied Brent Geese regularly wintered in Chichester Harbour and possibly in Pagham Harbour, though little quantitative data are available for either location. Following the global trend, numbers in Sussex dwindled, with birds ceasing to winter there on a regular basis by the early 1950s. At Chichester and Pagham Harbours, the wintering flock became re-established from the mid 1950s with a marked increase through the 1960s. By the 1970s, numbers in both Harbours were considered to be higher than ever before (Shrubb 1979). Chichester Harbour was, as suggested previously, favoured during the period of re-establishment with 25 birds in 1952/53 rising quickly to 220 in 1955/56, but then falling below 300 until 1960/61. At Pagham Harbour, the winter peak count did not exceed 200 birds until the winter of 1973/74, but was 1,030 by 1975/76. It is evident that the Sussex Harbours, together with the adjacent east Hampshire Harbours, acted as nuclei for re-establishment in Britain following the low point of the early 1950s (Rowcliffe & Mitchell 1998). Since winter 1973/74, birds have fed extensively on the grazing marshes adjacent to the Harbours as well as on intertidal beds of *Enteromorpha* and *Zostera*.

2.1.6.3   Internationally important sites

i) Chichester Harbour

Five-year mean 95/96-99/2000: 9,120

Site conservation status
SPA (Chichester and Langstone Harbours: selection stage 1.2)
Ramsar (Chichester and Langstone Harbours)
SSSI (Chichester Harbour)
IBA (Chichester and Langstone Harbours: criteria A4i, B1i & C3)

Site description and habitat
Chichester Harbour (SU7700) is an intertidal basin with river valleys forming four major arms to the north. In the western arm, the site is joined to Langstone Harbour by a stretch of water that separates Hayling Island from the mainland. At low tide, extensive areas of sand and mudflats are exposed that support beds of *Zostera* and *Enteromorpha*, the extent and distribution of these beds having varied during the review period (A. Potier pers. comm.).

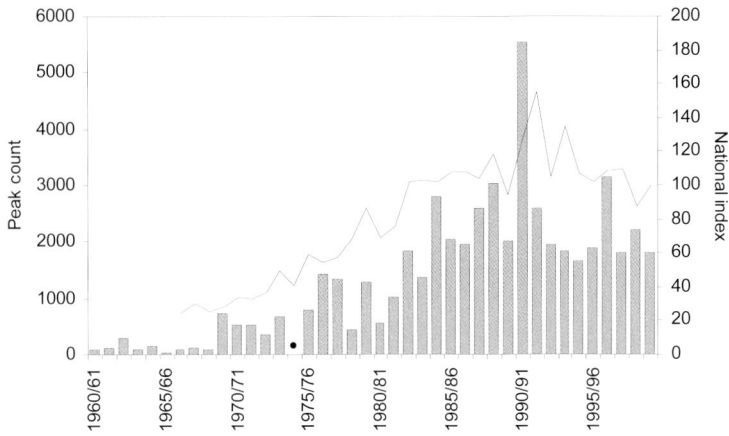

Fig. 34. Dark-bellied Brent Geese at the Swale Estuary, 1960/61-1999/2000: peak counts (bars) and British index (line) (circles denote years with no known data)

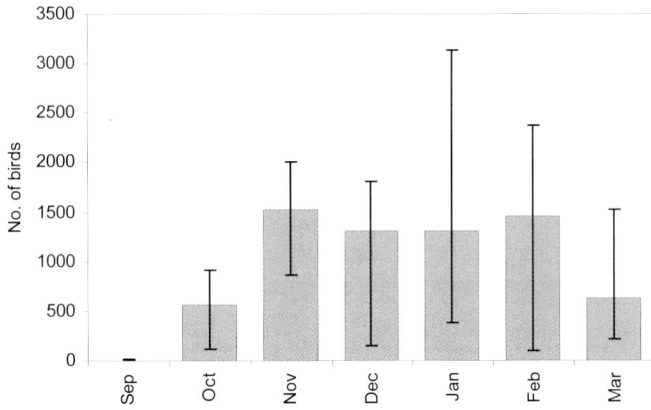

Fig. 35. Dark-bellied Brent Geese at the Swale Estuary, 1995/96-1999/2000: mean peak counts by month (error bars denote minimum and maximum peak counts during the period)

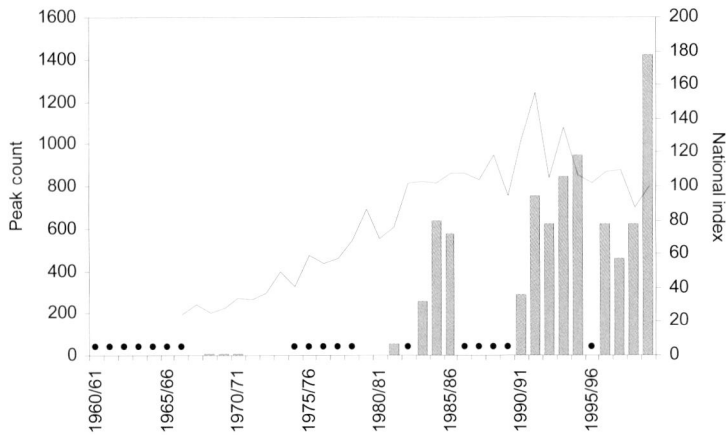

Fig. 36. Dark-bellied Brent Geese at Thanet Coast, 1960/61-1999/2000: peak counts (bars) and British index (line) (circles denote years with no known data)

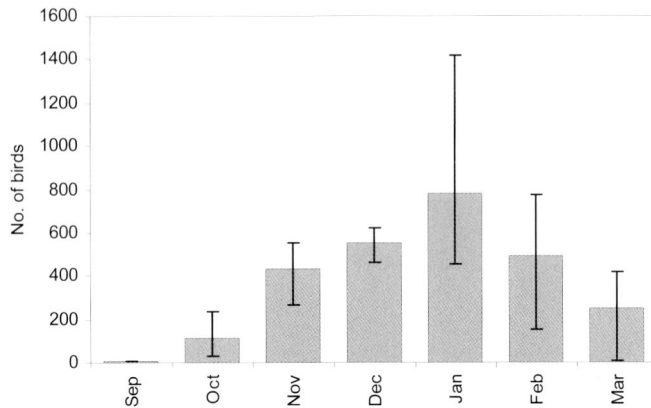

Fig. 37. Dark-bellied Brent Geese at Thanet Coast, 1995/96-1999/2000: mean peak counts by month (error bars denote minimum and maximum peak counts during the period)

Saltmarsh is extensive throughout the estuary, with large areas of *Spartina* dominating the lower tidal levels. Though much of the shoreline is undeveloped, the estuary has been subject to substantial land-claim with much of it fronted by sea walls behind which are small areas of grazing marshes. The majority of the hinterland is arable farmland.

Numbers and trends
In recent winters, peak counts of between 8,000 – 11,000 birds have been recorded either in January or February (Fig. 38 and 39). Birds arrive during October and November when over 50% of peak winter numbers are present. Numbers are much lower by March when spring passage peaks along the Sussex coast (Shrubb 1979). Few birds remain into April.

Site use
During the WeBS Low Tide Counts of winter 1993/4, the majority of Dark-bellied Brent Geese were recorded in the western half of the site, between Thorney and Hayling Island, where they feed on fields in late winter (Cranswick *et al.* 1995). In contrast, repeat surveys in subsequent years found flocks to be widely dispersed across the site with the largest concentration along the southeast shore at Rookwood in 1997/98 (Cranswick *et al.* 1999, Pollitt *et al.* 2000).

2.1.6.4   Nationally important sites

i) Pagham Harbour

Five-year mean 95/96-99/2000: 2,133

Site conservation status
SPA (Pagham Harbour: non-qualifying species)
Ramsar (Pagham Harbour: non-qualifying species)
SSSI (Pagham Harbour)
IBA (Pagham Harbour: criteria B1i & C3)

Site description and habitat
Pagham Harbour (SZ8796) is a small basin (266 ha) of extensive intertidal mudflats and saltmarsh surrounded by brackish marsh and pasture. The latter areas are the consequence of much agricultural land-claim around the estuary that has also led to little upper saltmarsh development. *Spartina* dominates almost half of the lower saltmarsh communities. Shingle spits across the estuary's mouth protect the tidal basin from the sea and provide a narrow entrance.

Numbers and trends
Site phenology is similar to that at the adjacent Chichester Harbour though the numbers of birds remaining in March can be over 50% of the peak count for a winter. The peak count is typically of 1,000–3,000 birds occurring in either January or February, after a variable build-up between October and December (Fig. 40 and 41).

Site use
Dark-bellied Brent Geese can be widely dispersed at low tide, but concentrate to graze in fields to the north of Pagham Wall, at the north end of the site (Cranswick *et al.* 1997, Waters *et al.* 1998, Cranswick *et al.* 1999, Pollitt *et al.* 2000). Fields inland of Sidlesham Ferry and Church Norton are regularly used, as noted in a study that documented a switch from winter cereals to pasture during November and December (McKay *et al.* 1994). The saltmarshes adjacent to these areas also support notable concentrations of birds in some years. Birds roost nocturnally within Pagham Harbour (McKay *et al.* 1994).

2.1.6.5   Key references

Shrubb (1979).

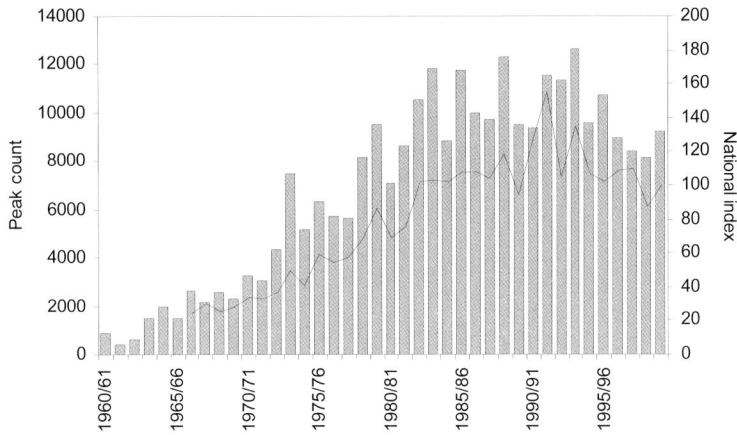

Figure 38. Dark-bellied Brent Geese at Chichester Harbour, 1960/61-1999/2000: peak counts (bars) and British index (line) (circles denote years with no known data)

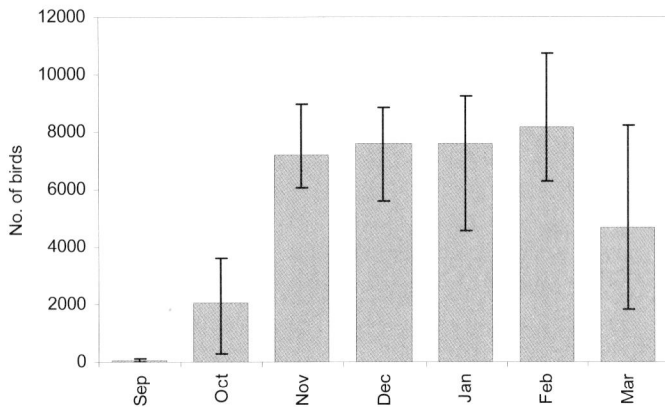

Figure 39. Dark-bellied Brent Geese at Chichester Harbour, 1995/96-1999/2000: mean peak counts by month (error bars denote minimum and maximum peak counts during the period)

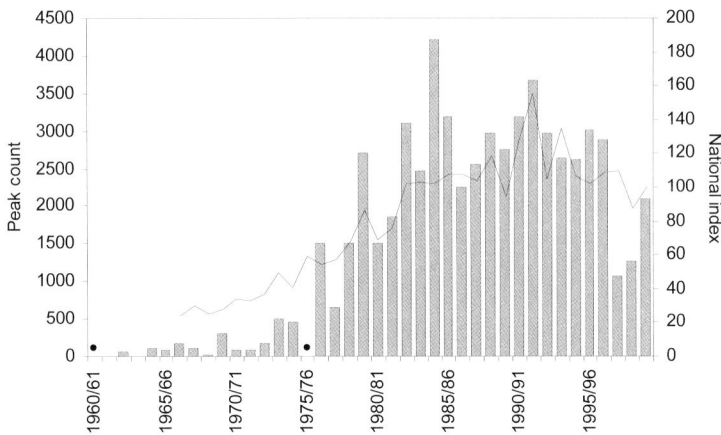

Figure 40. Dark-bellied Brent Geese at Pagham Harbour, 1960/61-1999/2000: peak counts (bars) and British index (line) (circles denote years with no known data)

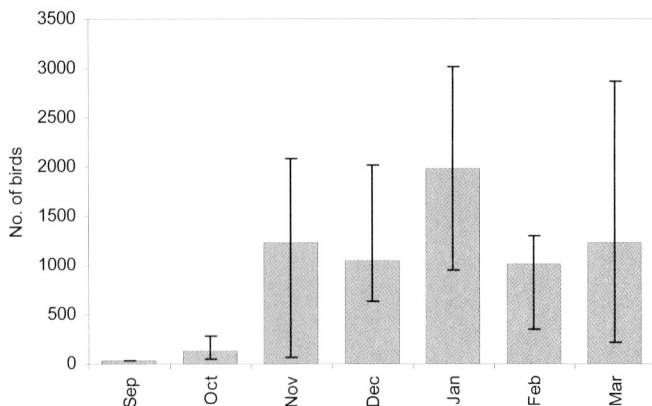

Figure 41. Dark-bellied Brent Geese at Pagham Harbour, 1995/96-1999/2000: mean peak counts by month (error bars denote minimum and maximum peak counts during the period)

2.1.7   The Solent

2.1.7.1   Background

This region of the English south coast has seen intensive human use in the low-lying coastal plain where there has been substantial loss and damage to the extensive estuarine habitat. Urban and industrial development encircles the two natural harbours of Portsmouth and Langstone in the east, and along much of Southampton Water. Naval and commercial ports amongst associated developments dominate these sites with the associated large urban populations each exceeding 50,000 persons (Buck 1997). To the west, the New Forest lies adjacent to the coast through which the River Beaulieu meanders prior to entering the sea via a narrow estuary. At the region's western extremity along the northwest Solent coast lies the estuary of Lymington river whose upper reach is fronted by the town of Lymington. Agriculture within the shadow of the New Forest largely dominates the landscape of this coast west of the immediate environs of Southampton Water. The Isle of Wight forms the southern shore of the Solent where in conservation terms the most important estuary is that of the Newtown River in the west. Elsewhere along the island's north coast, four small coastal plain estuaries break the coastline of sandy bays, unstable cliffs and varying expanses of intertidal flats, backed by a landscape of agriculture and small towns.

2.1.7.2   Historical status

Kelsall and Munn's publication of 1905, *The Birds of Hampshire and the Isle of Wight,* indicated that the Dark-bellied Brent Goose was a common winter visitor to the coast (Cohen 1963). Though quantitative data on the global decline in the species locally is absent, its revival is patchily documented, the Langstone Harbour winter peak increasing from 70 birds in 1952/53 to 750 by 1957/58 (Cohen 1963). This site would appear to be the nuclei of the south coast Dark-bellied Brent Goose wintering group, numbers having reached a plateau in the mid 1980s. By this time, flocks in adjacent estuaries were well established and increasing from the 1970s, the rate of progress varying between sites. The inference that Portsmouth Harbour was also a population nuclei, as a consequence of the regional grouping made by Rowcliffe & Mitchell (1999), would appear to be unfounded from inspection of the WeBS data. Since the late 1990s, numbers may have declined at key sites in the region, following the national trend (Gregory *et al.* 2002b).

When birds first arrive at the sites in early winter, by preference they feed upon the intertidal beds of *Zostera* until late December. By then depletion and natural die-back of the plant causes a shift and foraging is then concentrated upon the beds of *Enteromorpha* intertidally and, since early 1970s, on neighbouring pasture, playing fields and cereal fields, mostly within 200 m of the shore (Owen *et al.* 1986). In recent winters, some birds have been recorded feeding on grassland sites shortly after their arrival (Aspinall & Tasker 1992). The many thousands of birds now foraging inland has resulted in agricultural conflict, as discussed earlier in this report. Aspinall & Tasker (1992) suggest flocks at each site within the Solent remain separate from each other throughout the winter and also show a strong between-year site fidelity.

2.1.7.3   Internationally important sites

ii) Langstone Harbour

Five-year mean 95/96-99/2000: 6,247

Site conservation status
SPA (Chichester and Langstone Harbours: selection stage 1.2)
Ramsar (Chichester and Langstone Harbours)
SSSI (Langstone Harbour)
IBA (Chichester and Langstone Harbours: criteria A4i, B1i & C3)

Site description and habitat
Langstone Harbour (SU6902)is a rectangular tidal basin surrounded on three sides by urban development though with much of the land adjacent to the shore remaining relatively open. The fourth, east side of the basin is the farmland of Hayling Island that separates the harbour from Chichester Harbour other than for a stretch of water in the northeast corner separating Hayling from the mainland. Extending out from the northern shore is Farlington Marsh, a peninsula of coastal grassland and marsh enclosed by sea walls. Offshore from Farlington lie four islands fringed by the Harbour's most extensive areas of saltmarsh, a large proportion dominated by *Spartina*. Throughout the Harbour, extensive mudflats colonised by beds of *Zostera* dominate the site intertidally, these becoming sandy near the narrow sea entrance as formed by two shingle bars. Eutrophication from sewage effluent has resulted in substantial developments of *Enteromorpha* mats intertidally.

Numbers and trends
The main arrival occurs during October with numbers remaining high from November through to March (Fig. 42 and 43). The peak count of 5,000 –

7,000 typically occurs in January, though can vary by a month. A variable but low number of birds remain in the estuary into April.

Site use
Farlington Marshes provides a relatively disturbance-free area for grazing Dark-bellied Brent Geese and, as a consequence, birds occur here in large numbers at low tide (Cranswick *et al.* 1995, Pollitt *et al.* 2000). Furthermore, a freshwater lake at Farlington Marsh also allows birds to bath and drink (P. Potts pers. comm.). Extensive use is also made of sport fields adjacent and landward of Farlington Marsh (P. Potts pers. comm., Hampshire Brent Goose Strategy Group 2001). *Enteromorpha* and *Zostera* on the mudflats adjacent to Budds Sewage Farm also concentrates birds. Otherwise, birds are distributed widely within the estuary.

2.1.7.4   Nationally important sites

i) Portsmouth Harbour

Five-year mean 95/96-99/2000: 2,579

Site conservation status
SPA (Portsmouth Harbour: selection stage 1.2)
Ramsar (Portsmouth Harbour)
SSSI (Portsmouth Harbour)
IBA (Portsmouth Harbour: criterion C7)

Site description and habitat
Portsmouth Harbour (SU6204) is a tidal basin where low tide exposes large expanses of intertidal flats, predominately of mud, and tidal creeks. The mudflats support large beds of *Zostera* and expansive mats of *Enteromorpha*. Some large areas of saltmarsh exist, these dominated by *Spartina*. Freshwater input is limited and principally from the River Wallington via the Fareham Creek that forms an arm from the northwest corner arm of the Harbour. The Harbour has been the subject of piecemeal land claim, the shores having been built up with extensive port and housing developments that also border the comparatively narrow sea entrance. However, to the west lies protected land owned by the Ministry of Defence.

Numbers and trends
The main arrival occurs during October with large numbers present from November through to March. The timing of the annual peak count of 2,000 – 3,000 birds is highly variable (Fig. 44 and 45). Birds leave the site in March, with very few using the site during April.

Site use
At low tide, the species was found to be widely dispersed through the site during the winter of 1997/98 with low densities in the outer central mudflats (Cranswick *et al.* 1999).

ii) Southampton Water

Five-year mean 95/96-99/2000: 2,200

Site conservation status
SPA (Solent and Southampton Water: selection stage 1.2)
Ramsar (Solent and Southampton Water)
NNR (Titchfield Haven)
SSSI (various)
IBA (Southampton Water and Solent Marshes: criteria A4i, B1i & C3)

Site description and habitat
Southampton Water (SU4507) encompasses the tidal reaches of the Rivers Hamble, Test and Itchen and their confluence into one broad, largely subtidal channel, Southampton Water, which extends downstream of Southampton to its mouth with the Solent at Calshot and Titchfield Haven. The site is highly developed with dock and port facilities dominating a shoreline that includes a Power Station, Oil Refinery and the urban sprawl of Southampton and its conurbations. However, some areas of wet pasture and freshwater marsh backed by wet meadows remain, including Dibden and Titchfield Haven. Flanking the channels are intertidal flats of predominately mud with varying proportions of gravel. Areas of saltmarsh remain throughout the estuary at various levels, the large area between Hythe and Calshot including extensive areas of *Spartina*.

Figure 42. Dark-bellied Brent Geese at Langstone Harbour, 1960/61-1999/2000: peak counts (bars) and British index (line) (circles denote years with no known data)

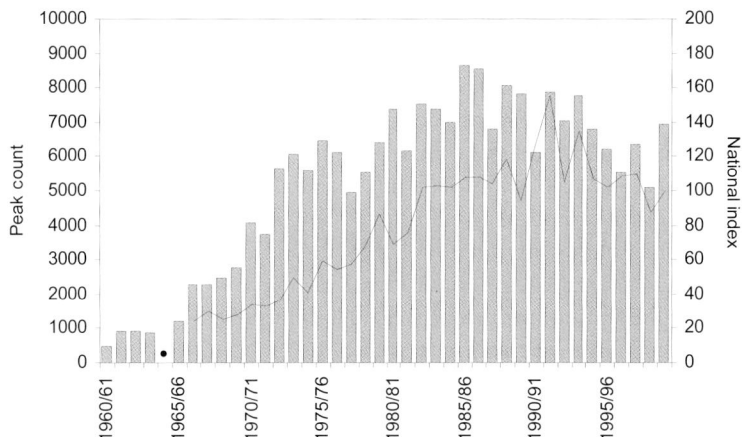

Figure 43. Dark-bellied Brent Geese at Langstone Harbour, 1995/96-1999/2000: mean peak counts by month (error bars denote minimum and maximum peak counts during the period)

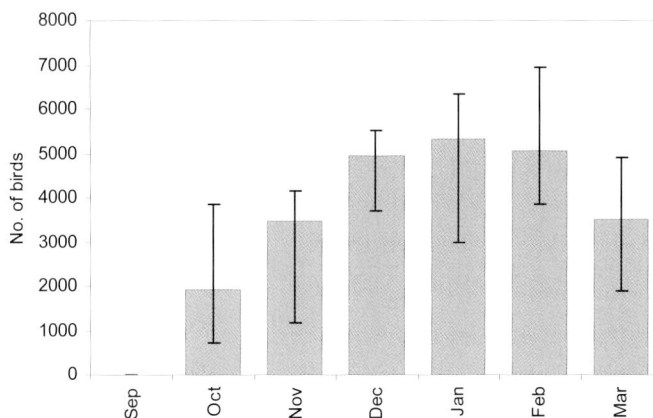

Figure 44. Dark-bellied Brent Geese at Portsmouth Harbour, 1960/61-1999/2000: peak counts (bars) and British index (line) (circles denote years with no known data)

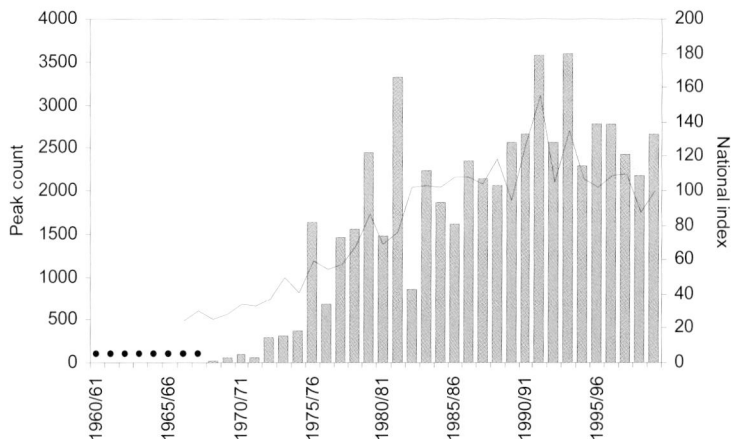

Figure 45. Dark-bellied Brent Geese at Portsmouth Harbour, 1995/96-1999/2000: mean peak counts by month (error bars denote minimum and maximum peak counts during the period)

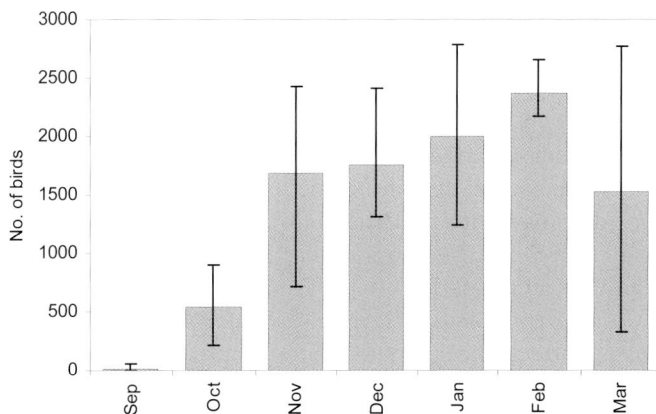

41

Numbers and trends

Birds arrive during October with the timing and size of the seasonal peak count highly variable between years. Annual peaks of 800–3,000 birds have been recorded between November and February (Fig. 46 and 47). The majority of these birds remain on site through to March, few using the site thereafter.

Site use

Dark-bellied Brent Geese occur widely through the estuary with most birds concentrated on both shores downstream of Hamble-le-Rice and Fawley (Cranswick *et al.* 1997, Waters *et al.* 1998, Pollitt *et al.* 2000). Upstream, the Dibden Bay foreshore generally supports highest densities. Aspinall & Tasker (1992) state that birds from Southampton Water roost overnight outside of the site at Calshot.

iii) Beaulieu Estuary

Five-year mean 95/96-99/2000: 1,853

Site conservation status

SPA (Solent and Southampton Water: selection stage 1.2)
Ramsar (Solent and Southampton Water)
NNR (North Solent)
SSSI (North Solent)
IBA (Southampton Water and Solent Marshes: criteria A4i, B1i & C3)

Site description and habitat

This site is centred upon the relatively long and narrow estuary of the meandering Beaulieu River (SZ4298). Narrow mudflats backed by saltmarsh, predominately *Spartina*, are exposed at low tide along the channels length. At its mouth with the Solent, the channel is diverted eastwards by the shingle spits of Needs Ore Point that provide shelter to the largest expanse of saltmarsh at Exbury Head. At the mouth, foreshore continues southwest to Colgrims and northeast to Calshot Castle prior to which are the mudflats at Stanwood Bay. The mudflats of both Stanwood Bay and the Beaulieu channel support extensive beds of *Zostera*. Sea walls and woodland bound the channel, whilst inland to the west are some wet meadows and marshes.

Numbers and trends

Numbers build up during October with further increases prior to a January/February peak of 1,200 – 2,500 birds (Fig. 48 and 49). By April, numbers fall to around a third of the annual peak, with up to 500 birds still using the site in to May.

Site use

The most important areas for feeding are the extensive grasslands and coastal grazing marshes on Warren Farm, Park Farm and Park Shore, to the west of the Beaulieu River, where birds spend most of the daylight hours (R. Lord pers. comm., Waters *et al.* 1998). Some birds roost on the sea off Gull Island at the estuary mouth, up-ending there to feed at low tide (Aspinall & Tasker 1992). Birds from Southampton Water also roost overnight at Calshot (Aspinall & Tasker 1992).

iv) Northwest Solent

Five-year mean 95/96-99/2000: 2,501

Site conservation status

SPA (Solent and Southampton Water: selection stage 1.2)
Ramsar (Solent and Southampton Water)
SSSI (Hurst Castle and Lymington River Estuary)
IBA (Southampton Water and Solent Marshes: criteria A4i, B1i & C3)

Site description and habitat

Immediately west of the Beaulieu Estuary, the foreshore of this 1,367 ha site (SZ3395) extends southwest to the mile long shingle spit of Hurst Castle, the pivotal feature being the Lymington Estuary. This coastal plain estuary is bordered by the town of Lymington on the west bank, the channel short and rapidly opening out to a broad mouth. Saltmarsh dominated by *Spartina* covers the vast majority of the 589 ha of intertidal, extending along the foreshores and up the river channel, open mudflats comprising of less than 15% of the area. Inland of the sea walls are extensive grazing marshes and lagoons.

Numbers and trends

Numbers build up during October, peaking at any time between November and January at 2,000 to 3,000 birds (Fig. 50 and 51). The majority of birds remain through to March with fewer than 100 using the site by April.

Site use

Though widespread, a WeBS Low Tide Count in 1997/98 (Cranswick *et al.* 1999) found the majority of birds at the site concentrated south of Keyhaven

.

Figure 46. Dark-bellied Brent Geese at Southampton Harbour, 1960/61-1999/2000: peak counts (bars) and British index (line) (circles denote years with no known data)

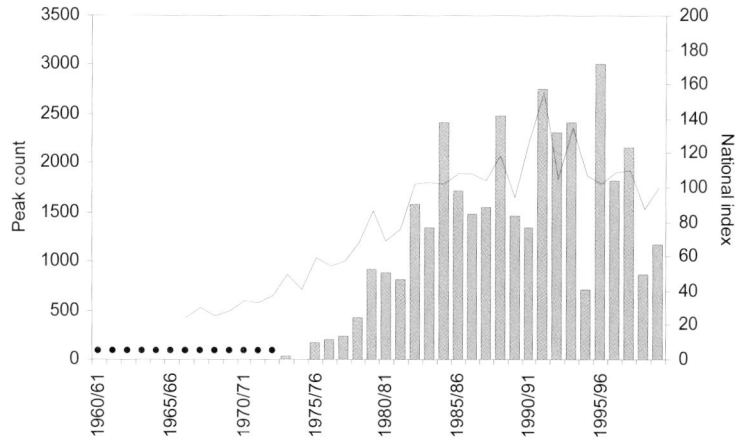

Figure 47. Dark-bellied Brent Geese at Southampton Harbour 1995/96-1999/2000: mean peak counts by month (error bars denote minimum and maximum peak counts during the period)

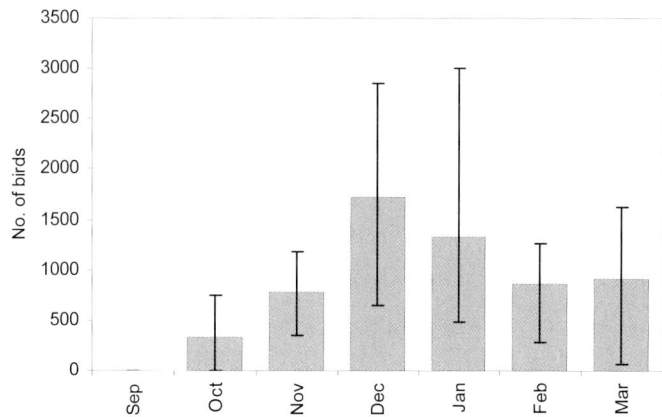

Figure 48. Dark-bellied Brent Geese at Beaulieu Estuary, 1960/61-1999/2000: peak counts (bars) and British index (line) (circles denote years with no known data)

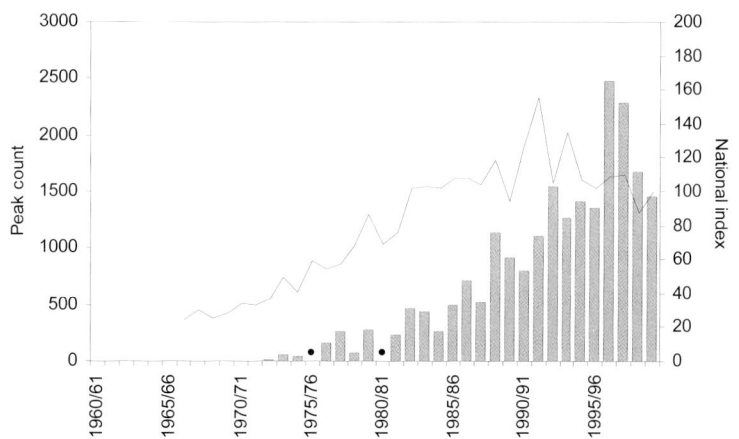

Figure 49. Dark-bellied Brent Geese at Beaulieu Estuary, 1995/96-1999/2000: mean peak counts by month (error bars denote minimum and maximum peak counts during the period)

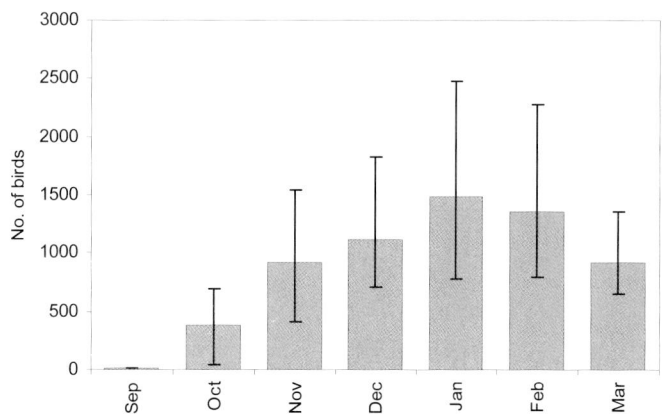

v) Newtown Estuary

Five-year mean 95/96-99/2000: 1,514

Site conservation status
SPA (Solent and Southampton Water: selection stage 1.2)
Ramsar (Solent and Southampton Water)
NNR (Newtown Harbour)
SSSI (Newtown Harbour)
IBA (Southampton Water and Solent Marshes: criteria A4i, B1i & C3)

Site description and habitat
The 332 ha estuary of the River Newtown and its tributaries is the largest estuary on the Isle of Wight and is situated half way along the island's northwest coast (SZ4291). Convoluted creeks feed into the shallow estuary of extensive intertidal flats that includes mud some of which support beds of *Enteromorpha* and *Zostera*. Mature saltmarshes fringe the creeks whilst more recently developed marshes and intertidal flats are found within a large central area that was previously grazing marsh until a sea-wall breach in 1954. Two shingle bars across the estuary mouth form a narrow exit into the Solent. Outside, the site's open coast is of mud and shingle intertidal areas backed by soft cliffs extending east to Gurnard Ledge.

Numbers and trends
Only small numbers birds have arrived on the estuary by October with the majority present through November to February. Some birds leave the site by March. The peak winter count is typically made in December or January, of between 1,100 and 1,800 birds (Fig. 52 and 53).

Site use
Flocks within the site occasionally wander outside the main estuary to forage at Thorness Bay (Aspinall & Tasker 1992). Indeed, low water coverage of the estuary in 1999/2000 by WeBS Low Tide Counts found birds to be widely distributed but with some preference for the central parts, in particular Causeway Lake (Musgrove *et al.* 2001).

2.1.7.5   Key references

Cohen (1963), Aspinall & Tasker (1992).

2.1.8   Dorset

2.1.8.1   Background

The Dorset coast is largely undeveloped with long stretches of coast where public access is only possible by foot. East from the coastal heaths of Studland, the coast comprises a series of relatively shallow sandy bays separated from each by prominent headlands of differing geology. Between the two shallow natural harbours of Poole and Christchurch stretches the main centre of populace, Poole, Bournemouth and Christchurch. Extending west from Poole Basin for around 30 km to Weymouth Bay is the Isle of Purbeck, a landscape of chalk and limestone cliffs backed by chalk downland agriculture. On the opposite side of the low-lying coast of Weymouth Bay is the limestone cliff edged Isle of Portland. This coast is where the region's other coastal centre of populace lies, Weymouth, that largely surrounds the freshwater lagoon and grazing marshes of Radipole and Lodmoor. Landward, Portland shelters 10 km^2 of waters within Portland Harbour this area also enclosed by man-made breakwaters and to the west, Chesil Bank. Chesil Bank is a 13 km shingle bar running west to Abbotsbury that separates Britain's largest tidal lagoon from the sea other than at its mouth into Portland Harbour at Ferrybridge. The Fleet and Portland Harbour provide the regions only estuarine habitat west of the Isle of Purbeck.

2.1.8.2   Historical status

In the late 19th century, the pressure from punt gunning in Poole Harbour apparently resulted in Dark-bellied Brent Geese relocating to Studland Bay outside the Harbour by day (Mansel-Pleydell 1888), flighting at dusk to forage (Prendergast & Boys 1983). As for the numbers involved, the species is said to have been numerous before 1939 with 200 at Weymouth Bay and hundreds in Poole Harbour in 1929 (Prendergast & Boys 1983, Owen *et al.* 1986). With the wasting of *Zostera* in the 1930s, numbers of birds in Poole Harbour declined markedly with only up to 25 birds recorded from the late 1940s to early 1960s. Numbers have since increased with over 200 birds at Poole Harbour and Fleet/Wey by 1973/74 and 1980/81 respectively. Of note, but as yet unexplained, is the substantial increase in numbers at both sites from winter 1990/91 onwards. Since the late 1970s, the species has also begun frequenting Christchurch Harbour on a regularly basis.

Figure 50. Dark-bellied Brent Geese at Northwest Solent, 1960/61-1999/2000: peak counts (bars) and British index (line) (circles denote years with no known data)

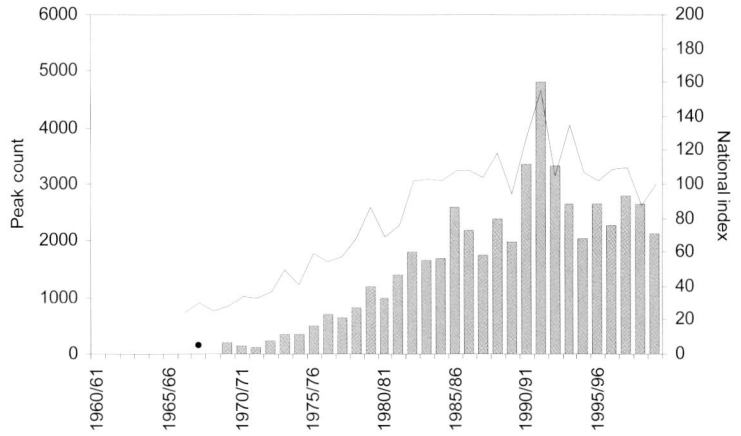

Figure 51. Dark-bellied Brent Geese at Northwest Solent, 1995/96-1999/2000: mean peak counts by month (error bars denote minimum and maximum peak counts during the period)

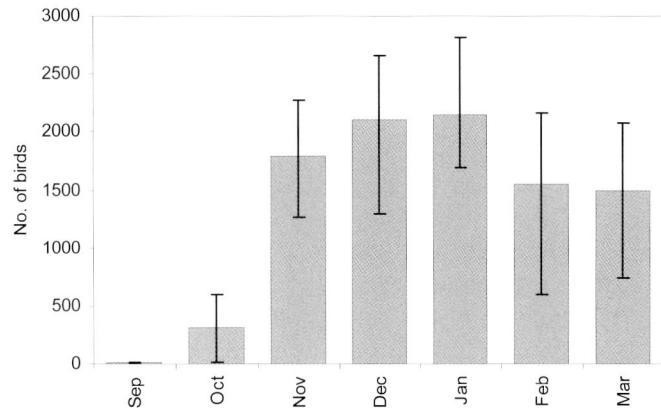

Figure 52. Dark-bellied Brent Geese at Newtown Estuary, 1960/61-1999/2000: peak counts (bars) and British index (line) (circles denote years with no known data)

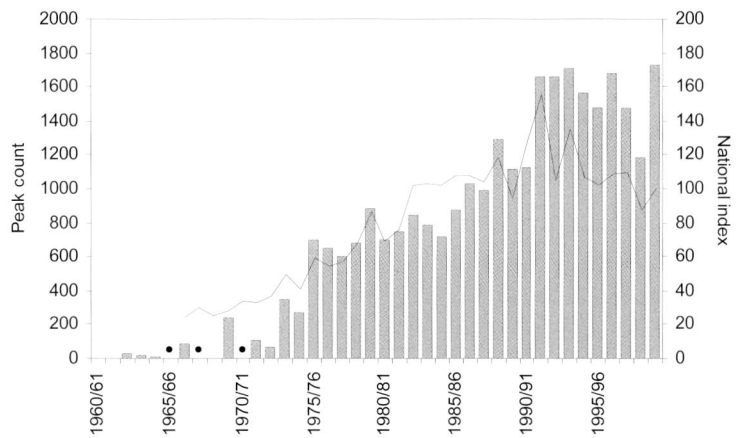

Figure 53. Dark-bellied Brent Geese at Newtown Estuary, 1995/96-1999/2000: mean peak counts by month (error bars denote minimum and maximum peak counts during the period)

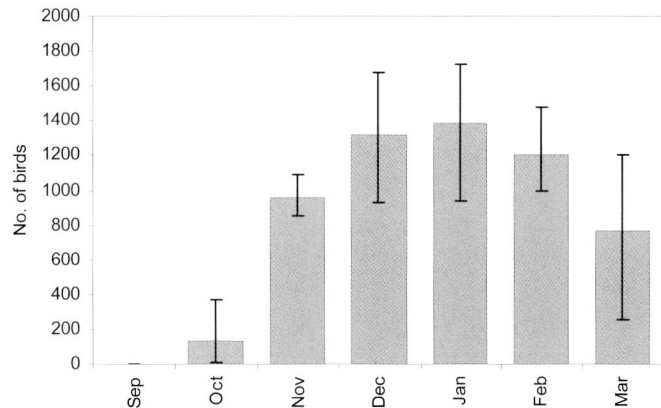

2.1.8.3   Nationally important sites

i) Poole Harbour

Five-year mean 95/96-99/2000: 1,441

Site conservation status
SPA (Poole Harbour: selection stage 1.3)
Ramsar (Poole Harbour)
NNR (Studland and Godlington Heaths, Arne)
SSSI (various)
IBA (Poole Harbour: non-listed species)

Site description and habitat
Poole Harbour (SY9988), the world's largest natural harbour at 3,805 ha, is a drowned valley with higher land remaining as islands and promontories. The River Frome and Piddle flow into this shallow tidal basin at its north-west corner. The double ebb and flow tide generated from the Solent coast provides a complex tidal cycle within the Harbour. At low tide, extensive areas of mudflats supporting *Zostera* beds are exposed largely along the western and convoluted south shores, Holes Bay and Lytchett Bay. Saltmarshes dominated by *Spartina*, also fringe these same shores. In the east, two low-lying sand spits form a narrow 400 m wide sea entrance into Poole Bay. The urban and port developments of Poole and Bournemouth along the north shore east of Lytchett Bay, contrast with the largely protected south shore of heaths, forestry and some wet meadows e.g. Wareham Meadows SSSI.

Numbers and trends
Arrival occurs during October and November. Typically, numbers peak sometime between December and February at 1,200–1,700 birds (Fig. 54 and 55). However, within this period and into March, numbers counted can fall to below 50% of the peak count suggesting interchange between this and sites elsewhere. Few birds use the site beyond March.

Site use
Though birds feed throughout the estuary, preference is shown for the undisturbed and sheltered bays between Studland and Arne (Aspinall & Tasker 1990, Cranswick *et al*. 1995).

ii) Fleet/Wey

Five-year mean 95/96-99/2000: 2,580

Site conservation status
SPA (Chesil Beach and The Fleet: selection stage 1.2)
Ramsar (Chesil Beach and The Fleet)
SSSI (Portland Harbour Shore, Chesil and The Fleet)
IBA (Chesil Beach and The Fleet: criteria B1i & C3)

Site description and habitat
The Fleet (SY6976) is a long and very shallow lagoon that becomes less tidal and saline with distance from the narrow sea entrance at the southeast end into Portland Harbour. At low tide, the site's main expanse of 227 ha of mud and sand flats, are within the small inner bay of Portland Harbour at Ferrybridge and the southeastern part of the very shallow Fleet. The Fleet supports extensive beds of *Zostera*. Only small areas of intertidal mudflats are present within the larger outer part of Portland Harbour. Saltmarsh is confined to narrow strips along both sides of the Fleet, the seaward boundary being the shingle bar of Chesil Bank.

Numbers and trends
This site is unusual in that numbers typically peak during November with large flocks often present by October. Numbers fall to below 600 birds in January and December with rarely any individuals still present by April (Fig. 56 and 57).

Site use
The majority of birds use the Fleet with only a small proportion occasionally feeding in Portland Harbour e.g. at Ferrybridge (White & Webb 1995). Some foraging inland on cropped fields does now occur and is causing some concern.

2.1.8.4   Key references

Mansel-Pleydell (1888), Prendergast & Boys (1983), Aspinall & Tasker (1990), White & Webb (1995)

Figure 54. Dark-bellied Brent Geese at Poole
Harbour, 1960/61-1999/2000: peak
counts (bars) and British index
(line) (circles denote years with no
known data)

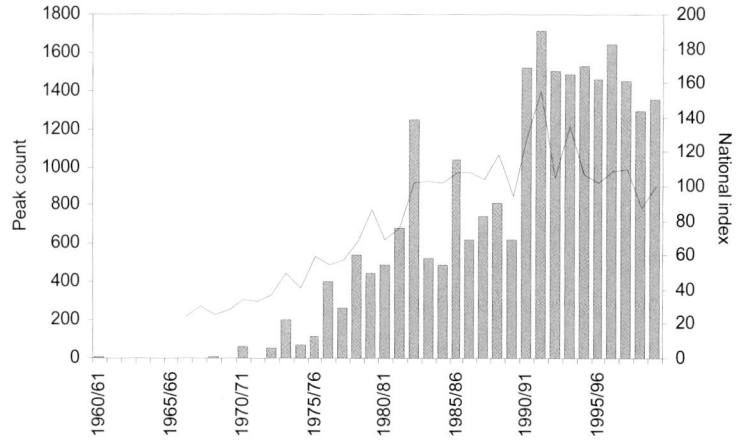

Figure 55. Dark-bellied Brent Geese at Poole
Harbour, 1995/96-1999/2000: mean
peak counts by month (error bars
denote minimum and maximum
peak counts during the period)

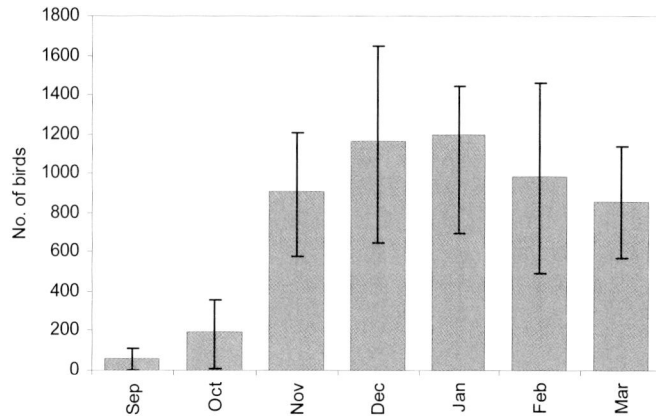

Figure 56. Dark-bellied Brent Geese at the
Fleet/Wey, 1960/61-1999/2000:
peak counts (bars) and British
index (line) (circles denote years
with no known data)

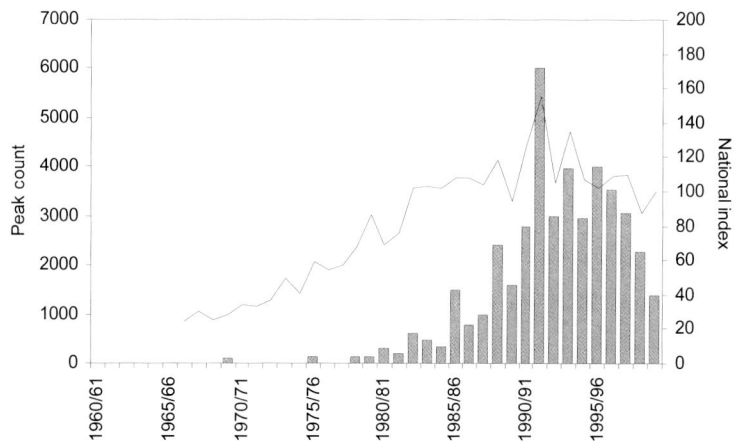

Figure 57. Dark-bellied Brent Geese at the
Fleet/Wey, 1995/96-1999/2000:
mean peak counts by month (error
bars denote minimum and
maximum peak counts during the
period)

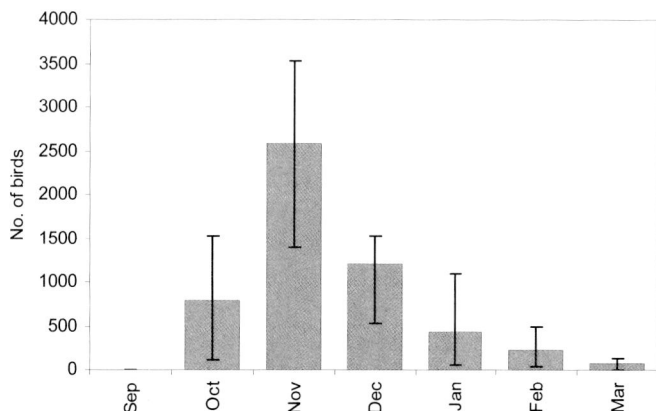

2.1.9   Devon

2.1.9.1   Background

The south Devon coast is for much of its length cliffs with those estuaries present generally drowned river valleys that are narrow, steeply-sided and for most comparatively small areas of mudflats, these situated in the upper reaches. The two estuaries that do support extensive mudflats are Plymouth Sound and the Exe. The latter estuaries also have surrounding populations that exceed 100,000 in contrast to the rather fewer people that live close to the remainder of the south Devon estuaries.

2.1.9.2   Historical status

In the early 1930s, Dark-bellied Brent Goose numbers on the Exe Estuary totalled up to 300 birds. With the wasting of *Zostera* in the 1930s, the species virtually disappeared at this site with fewer than 30 birds recorded annually during the early 1950s. Numbers increased to 120 birds during most of the 1960s. From 1968 until the late 1980s, numbers increased at a similar pace to that nationally, peaking within the range of 2,500–4,000 birds. A slow decline occurred in the 1990s, reflecting the national trend. Since 1978, wintering flocks have become established elsewhere, including the Kingsbridge Estuary and Plymouth Sound, although none have reached the importance of the Exe Estuary for the species (Owen *et al.* 1986).

2.1.9.3   Nationally important sites

i) Exe Estuary

Five-year mean 95/95 – 99/2000: 1,709

Site conservation status
SPA (Exe Estuary: selection stage 1.3)
Ramsar (Exe Estuary)
SSSI (Dawlish Warren, Exe Estuary)
IBA (Exe Estuary: non-listed species)

Site description and habitat
The Exe Estuary (SX9883) supports a diversity of estuarine habitats, extending over 10 km south from the city of Exeter to the open sea at Exmouth and Dawlish Warren. The latter is a sandy spit running east in to the estuary mouth and sheltering much of the site from the sea. Low tide reveals 60% of the 1,874 ha estuary to be intertidal flats predominately of mud and silt but becoming sandy in the lee of Dawlish Warren. The mudflats support extensive beds of *Zostera* and *Enteromorpha*. Saltmarsh has

developed within the shelter of Dawlish Warren and elsewhere patches occur along the inner estuary. Rough grazing marshes back the estuary in the north-west at Exminster marshes and north-east at Clyst and Bowling Green Marshes. The majority of the estuary is otherwise flanked by road, railway and urban developments.

Numbers and trends
Typically, a winter peak of 1,500 – 2,000 birds occurs in October or November. Numbers generally remain at around 1,000 birds until February when birds begin to leave the site in large numbers (Fig. 58 and 59). Only a few individuals remain by April.

Site use
During October-December, birds are largely confined to the lower estuary, where they feed on extensive beds of *Zostera* at Exmouth and Dawlish Warren. Upon the *Zostera* being depleted in mid winter, they move on to the grazing marshes at Exminster, Clyst and Bowling Green Marshes. Another important grassland grazing site is at Starcross, which is a golf practice course during the summer

2.2   Wales

2.2.1   West Glamorgan & South Dyfed

2.2.1.1   Background

Much of the urban and industrial centres bordering this coast are restricted to the two estuaries with deep water, the Burry Inlet and Milford Haven, and Swansea Bay with its conurbation of Swansea, Neath and Port Talbot. These localities are interspersed by the undeveloped coasts of cliff and sandy bays of the Pembrokeshire Coast National Park and Gower, and the remaining sand dune complexes of the low lying coasts, the largest of which fringes Carmarthen Bay. The estuarine areas of this coast are in decreasing size the Burry Inlet, Carmarthen Bay, Neath Estuary, Milford Haven, Tawe & Swansea Bay and Afan Estuary. The former two sites support the region's most extensive areas of intertidal flats, this being largely of sand at Carmarthen Bay.

2.2.1.2   Historical status

Historically, the Dark-bellied Brent Goose has always been a regular winter visitor to the Burry Inlet but never as common as now (Lovegrove *et al.* 1994). In the early 1900s, the species was uncommon in Glamorgan. By the 1930s, numbers had apparently increased with very small numbers recorded at the Burry Inlet. Following the die-back of *Zostera* in the 1930s, and the associated global decline in the Dark-bellied Brent Goose population, numbers on the Burry Inlet remained at below 40 birds through until the early 1970s. Thereafter, numbers rose from 87 in 1974 to 1,435 in winter 1991/92 and 1,520 birds in 1998/99. Elsewhere in the region, the occurrence of Dark-bellied Brent Geese has been regularly, if sporadically, recorded chiefly at Blackpill in Swansea Bay, where the racial distinction from the scarcer Light-bellied Brent Goose has been made in all available records. The numbers of Dark-bellied Brent Geese at Blackpill peaked in 1990/91 with 53 birds. Smaller numbers of birds frequent Blackpill during spring and autumn passage with peak counts of 13 (1984) and 25 (1975) birds respectively. The occurrences at Blackpill clearly mirror the large increases at the Burry Inlet from 1975 onwards. Early September records at Blackpill generally precede the arrival in the Burry Inlet. Large numbers have on occasions been reported from Milford Haven.

2.2.1.3   Nationally important sites

i) Burry Inlet

Five-year mean 95/96-99/2000: 1,069

Site conservation status
SPA (Burry Inlet: non-qualifying species)
Ramsar (Burry Inlet: non-qualifying species)
NNR
SSSI (various)
IBA (Burry Inlet: non-listed species)

Site description and habitat
The Burry Inlet (SS5096) is an estuary of contrasting shorelines; the northern shore dominated by the conurbations of Burry Port and Llanelli, and the southern shore largely rural except where intersected by the Industrial Estate, west of Penclawdd. The only natural habitats remaining on the heavily industrialised north shore are the dune system of Pembrey Burrows at the western end and the saltmarsh at Tir Morfa. Part of a dune complex, Whiteford Burrows, dominates the southern shore at the estuary mouth. This shoreline is otherwise an extensive area of grazed saltmarsh behind which lies agricultural land. 4,366 ha of intertidal flats predominately sand but grading to silt in the upper reaches, extend across the 9,524 ha estuary. Mussel beds or scars are another dominant feature of the intertidal areas. The most notable are located off Tir Morfa and the north-west edge of Whiteford Burrow. The estuary includes the tidal reaches of its main tributary, the Loughor, which is comparatively narrow and fringed by areas of saltmarsh. The extent of the latter is steadily increasing in a westerly direction with the encroachment of mudflat by various marsh grasses.

Numbers and trends
Dark-bellied Brent Geese generally arrive on the Burry Inlet from September, with numbers rising to a winter peak of 900 – 1,200 birds, typically recorded in January or February (Fig. 60 and 61). Numbers vary considerably during a season with no regular pattern discernable. During the period of establishment at the Burry Inlet, from the 1950s onwards, birds initially arrived late and departed early, but arrived progressively earlier and departed later as numbers increased in subsequent decades (Summers *et al.* 1996). Few birds remain on the estuary in April.

Site use
The outer southern estuary, Whiteford east to Llanrhidian, forms the core range with birds seen increasingly elsewhere as the population has increased (Prŷs-Jones *et al.* 1989). In the 1960s, when numbers were comparatively small, birds were concentrated at high water at Whiteford, in the Burry Pill off Berges Island, and on its eastern margins of the saltmarsh near Landimore Marsh (R.J. Howell pers. comm.). At low water, the birds feed on the *Zostera* and *Enteromorpha* on Whiteford Sands below Hills Tor. With the marked increase in the 1970s and 1980s, the birds had extended their feeding and roosting range further up the Burry to Wernffrwd and with the exceptional high peaks of the 1990s, to Penclawdd and subsequently to Berthlwyd, where birds fed on saltmarsh grasses at low water and neap tides (R.J. Howell pers. comm., Howells 1995, Hurford & Lansdown 1995). Most recently, the 2000s, numbers have declined in the upper reaches of the estuary in accordance with recent fall in numbers in the UK. (R.J. Howell pers. comm.). In the 1980s, the population rise was also noted to coincide with an increase in the grazing of saltmarsh by geese, the birds generally foraging across Landimore Marsh though also at times more widely along the southern shore (Prŷs-Jones *et al.* 1989).

2.2.1.4   Key references

Prŷs-Jones *et al.* (1989), Lovegrove *et al.* (1994).

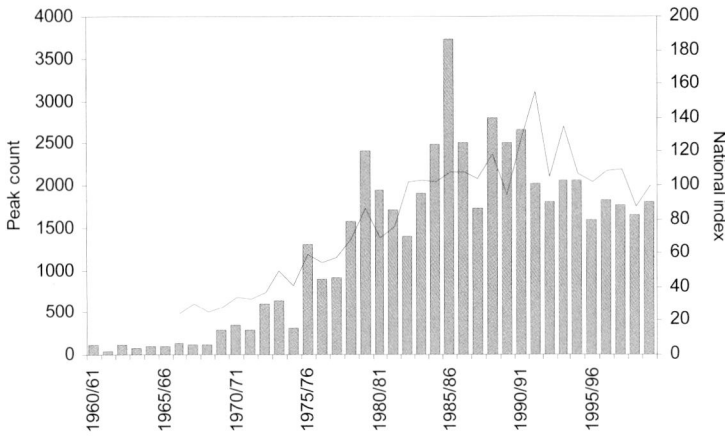

Figure 58. Dark-bellied Brent Geese at the Exe Estuary, 1960/61-1999/2000: peak counts (bars) and British index (line) (circles denote years with no known data)

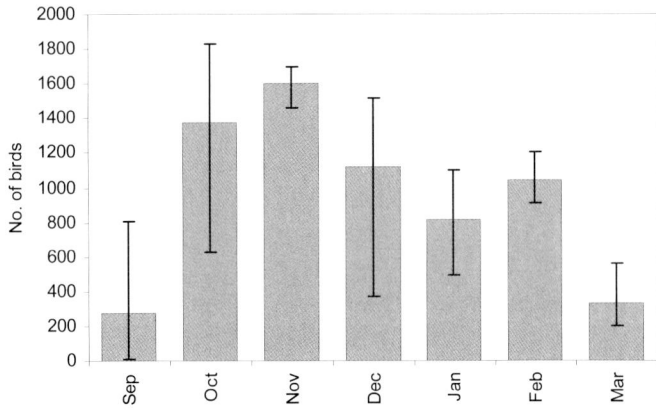

Figure 59. Dark-bellied Brent Geese at the Exe Estuary, 1995/96-1999/2000: mean peak counts by month (error bars denote minimum and maximum peak counts during the period)

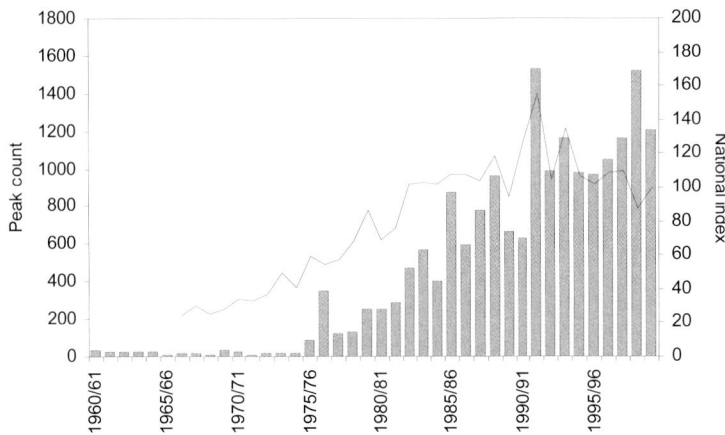

Figure 60. Dark-bellied Brent Geese at the Burry Inlet, 1960/61-1999/2000: peak counts (bars) and British index (line) (circles denote years with no known data)

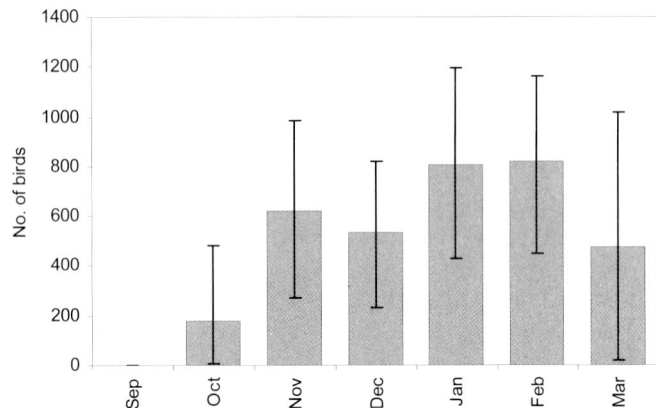

Figure 61. Dark-bellied Brent Geese at the Burry Inlet, 1995/96-1999/2000: mean peak counts by month (error bars denote minimum and maximum peak counts during the period)

3 FUTURE RESEARCH NEEDS

Although much is already known about the ecology and population dynamics of the Dark-bellied Brent Goose, there will always be a need to monitor the population in the face of continual change, not least that driven by global warming. We should strive to continue the on-going surveillance programmes e.g. WeBS, but as part of a broader Integrated Population Monitoring (IPM) programme for the species (Kershaw *et al.* 2001). This would benefit from increased effort on the individual marking of birds from across a broad suite of sites in the UK, as would the collation of productivity data. If a change in the hunting status of the Dark-bellied Brent Goose under the EC Birds Directive occurs as has been suggested, then an already established IPM integrating data from individually marked birds is a necessary tool for quantifying the impact of hunting and ensuring the sustainability of this goose population (Kershaw *et al.* 2001).

The surveillance of individually marked birds is an important pre-requisite for ensuring an adequate understanding of the functionality of the key sites and their integration. For example, a site may be much more important than is apparent from count data alone, as turnover rates at staging areas may be high (Evans 1984, Smit & Piersma 1989). This is particularly pertinent with the recent establishment of spring staging sites in Britain complementing the autumn staging site at Foulness. Frederiksen *et al.* (2001) provide a novel technique for estimating turnover based on counts and resightings of individually marked birds. The method could markedly improve our understanding of the true importance of staging sites where sightings as well as count data are available. The opportunity exists to apply this method in identifying those sites requiring statutory protection because of their importance to staging Dark-bellied Brent Geese.

It should be ensured that adequate surveillance at the key sites is given to the usage of agricultural feeding areas by Dark-bellied Brent Goose, these areas are not necessarily protected under any site-based designations but integral to the functionality of a site. Future awareness should also be focused upon monitoring changes in the temporal and spatial uses of the intertidal habitats, such that they reflect the condition of the resources available and the prevailing influence of disturbance upon the Dark-bellied Brent Goose population.

An important objective of future monitoring is that it should, in part, be aimed at underpinning the Flyway Management Plan for this population.

4   ACKNOWLEDGEMENTS

This review of monitoring information would not have been possible without the efforts of dedicated volunteer and professional ornithologists who monitor and research Dark-bellied Brent Geese throughout their range. The author is extremely grateful for their efforts and strongly encourages them to continue their valuable work into the future. The author would also like to thank Helen Baker, Colette Hall, Richard Hearn, James Robinson, Mark Pollitt, Nancy Robb, Paul Marshall and Peter Cranswick for their support and assistance during the production of this review and Marcus Rowcliffe who reviewed an earlier draft.

The author has made every effort to include all known data in this review. Given, however, that a number of unpublished reports and databases may have been overlooked, readers are urged to submit new and additional data to the author, especially where there are apparent gaps in the data sets use.

5 REFERENCES

Aspinall, S. & Tasker, M.L. 1990. *Coastal birds of east Dorset.* Seabirds Team, JNCC, Aberdeen.

Aspinall, S. & Tasker, M.L. 1992. *Birds of the Solent.* Seabirds Team, JNCC, Aberdeen.

Atkinson-Willes, G.L. & Matthews, G.V.T. 1960. The past status of the Brent Goose. *British Birds* 53: 352-357.

Barrett, R. 2002. Wildlife and Countryside Act 1981: *The monitoring of Brent Goose Licences. Annual Review of 2001-2002 season.* DEFRA report, Bristol.

Bergmann, H.-H., Stock, M. & Ten Thoren, B. 1994. *Ringelgänse, Arktische Gäste an unseren Küsten.* Aula-Verlag Wiesbaden.

Bianki, V.V. 1979. Status of *Branta Bernicla Bernicla* in White Sea passage areas, USSR. In: M. Smart (ed.) *Proceedings of the First Technical Meeting of Western Palearctic Migratory Bird Management*: 21-24. IWRB, Slimbridge.

Buck, A.L. 1993. *An inventory of UK estuaries. Volume 2. South-west Britain.* Peterborough, Joint Nature Conservation Committee.

Buck, A.L. 1997. *An inventory of UK estuaries Vol. 6: Southern England.* Peterborough, Joint Nature Conservation Committee.

Burd, F. 1992. *Erosion and vegetation change on the saltmarshes of Essex and north Kent between 1973 and 1988.* Peterborough, Nature Conservancy Council (Research and survey in nature conservation No. 42)

Charman, K. & Macey, A. 1978. The winter grazing of salt marsh vegetation by Dark-bellied Brent Geese. *Wildfowl* 29: 153-162.

Clark, J.A., Balmer, D.E, Blackburn, J.R., Milne, L.J., Robertson, R.A., Wernham, C.V., Adams, S.Y. & Griffin, B.M. 2002. Bird Ringing in Britain and Ireland in 2000. *Ringing & Migration* 21: 25-61.

Clausen, P. 1997. Dark-bellied Brent Geese *Branta b. bernicla* use of the White Sea. A progress report. In: J. van Nugteren (ed.) *Dark-bellied Brent Goose Branta bernicla bernicla Flyway Management Plan*: 174-183. Coproduction IKC Natuurbeheer No. C-17. Information and Reference Centre for Nature Management, Wageningen, The Netherlands.

Cohen, E. 1963. *Birds of Hampshire and the Isle of Wight.* Oliver & Boyd, London.

Cramp, S. & Simmons, K.E.L. 1977. *Birds of the Western Palearctic*, Vol 1, *Ostriches-Ducks*, Oxford University Press, Oxford.

Cranswick, P.A., Waters, R.J., Evans, J. & Pollitt, M.S. 1995. *The Wetland Bird Survey 1993-94: Wildfowl and Wader Counts.* BTO/WWT/RSPB/JNCC, Slimbridge.

Cranswick, P.A., Waters, R.J., Musgrove, A.J. & Pollitt, M.S. 1997. *The Wetland Bird Survey 1995-96: Wildfowl and Wader Counts.* BTO/WWT/RSPB/JNCC, Slimbridge.

Cranswick, P.A., Pollitt, M.S., Musgrove, A.J. & Hughes, R.C. 1999. *The Wetland Bird Survey 1997-98: Wildfowl and Wader Counts.* BTO/WWT/RSPB/JNCC, Slimbridge.

de Korte, J., Volkov, A.E. & Gavrilo, M.V. 1995. Bird Observations in Severnaya Zemlya, Siberia. *Arctic* 48: 222-234.

Ebbinge, B.S. 1989. A multifactorial explanation for variation in breeding performance of Brent Geese *Branta bernicla. Ibis* 131: 196-204.

Ebbinge, B.S. 1991. The impact of hunting on mortality rates and spatial distribution of geese, wintering in the Western Palearctic. *Ardea* 79: 197-209.

Ebbinge, B.S. 1992. Regulation of numbers of Dark-bellied Brent Goose *Branta bernicla bernicla* on spring staging sites. *Ardea* 80: 203-228.

Ebbinge, B.S. & St Joseph, A.K.M. 1992. The Brent Goose colour-ringing scheme: unravelling annual migratory movements from high arctic Siberia to the coasts of western Europe. In: B.S. Ebbinge. *Population Limitation in Arctic-breeding Geese*: 93-104. Published PhD thesis, University of Groningen.

Ebbinge, B.S. & Spaans, B. 1995. The importance of body-reserves accumulated in spring staging areas in the temperature zone for breeding of Dark-belied Brent Geese *Branta b. bernicla* in the high arctic. *Journal of Avian Biology* 26: 105-113.

Ebbinge, B.S. & Spaans, B. 2002. How do Brent Geese (*Branta b. bernicla*) cope with evil? Complex relationships between predator and prey. *Journal of Ornithology* 143: 33-42.

Ebbinge, B.S., Berrevoets, C., Clausen, P., Ganter, B., Günther, K., Koffjberg, K., Mahéo, R., Rowcliffe, M., St.Joseph, A.K.M., Südbeck, P. & Syroechkovsky Jr., E.E. 1999. Dark-bellied Brent Goose *Branta bernicla bernicla*. In: Madsen, J. & Cracknell, G. & Fox, A.D. (eds.) 1999. *Goose populations of the Western Palearctic. A review of status and distribution*: 284-297. Wetlands International Publ. No. 48, Wetlands International, Wageningen, The Netherlands. National Environmental Research Institute, Rönde, Denmark. 344 pp.

Ebbinge, B.S., Heesterbeek, J.A.P., Ens, B.J., & Goedhart, P.W. 2002. Density dependent population limitation in dark-bellied brent geese *Branta b. bernicla. Avian Science* 2: 63-75.

Evans, P.R. 1984. The British Isles. In: P.R. Evans, J.D. Goss-Custard. & W.G. Hale (eds.) *Coastal waders and wildfowl in winter*: 261-275. Cambridge University Press, Cambridge.

Filchagov, A.V. & Leonovich, V.V. 1992. Breeding range expansion of Barnacle and Brent Geese in the Russian –European North. *Polar Research* 11: 41-46.

Fox, A.D., Norriss, D.W., Stroud, D.A. & Wilson, H.J. 1994. *Greenland White-fronted Geese in Ireland and Britain 1982/83 - 1993/1994*. Greenland White-fronted Goose Study Research Report No. 8.

Frederiksen, M., Fox, A.D., Madsen, J. & Colhourn, K. 2001. Estimating the total number of birds using a staging site. *Journal of Wildlife Management* 65: 282-289.

Fredga, S. 1979. Status of *Branta bernicla bernicla* on passage in Sweden. In M. Smart (ed.) *Proceedings of the First Technical Meeting of Western Palearctic Migratory Bird Management* 30-32. IWRB, Slimbridge.

Glegg, W.M. 1929. *A History of the Birds of Essex*. Witherby, London.

Gibbs, G. 1993. Wildfowl & Waders of the Blackwater Estuary. *Essex Bird Report 1992*: 138-149.

Gillham, E.H. & Homes, R.C. 1950. *The Birds of the North Kent Marshes*. Collins, London.

Green, M., Alerstrom, T., Clausen, P., Drent, R. & Ebbinge, B.S. 2002a. Dark-bellied Brent Geese *Branta bernicla bernicla*, as recorded by satellite telemetry, do not minimize flight distance during spring migration. *Ibis* 144:106-121.

Green, M., Alerstrom, T., Clausen, P., Drent, R. & Ebbinge, B.S. 2002b. Site use by dark-bellied brent geese *Branta bernicla bernicla* on the Russian tundra as recorded by satellite telemetry: implications for East Atlantic Flyway conservation. *Wildlife Biology* 8: 229-239.

Gregory, R.D., Noble, D.G., Robinson, J.A., Stroud, D.A., Campbell, L.H., Rehfisch, M.M., Cranswick, P.A., Wilkinson, N.I., Crick, H.Q.P. & Green, R.E. 2002a. *The state of the UK's birds 2001*. RSPB, BTO, WWT and JNCC, Sandy.

Gregory, R.D., Wilkinson, N.I., Noble, D.G., Robinson, J.A., Brown, A.F., Hughes, J., Proctor, D., Gibbons, D.W. & Galbraith, C.A. 2002b. The population status of birds in the United Kingdom, Channel Islands and Isle of Man: an analysis of conservation concern 2002-2007. *British Birds* 95: 410-448.

Hampshire Brent Goose Strategy Group. 2001. *Brent Goose Strategy: south-east Hampshire coast*. Hampshire & Isle of Wight Wildlife Trust and Hampshire County Council.

Harrison, J.G. 1979. A new overland migration route of *Branta bernicla bernicla* in southeast England in autumn. In: M. Smart (ed.) *Proceedings of the First Technical Meeting of Western Palearctic Migratory Bird Management*. IWRB, Slimbridge.

Hearn, R.D. 2002. *The breeding success of Dark-bellied Brent Geese in 2001, as assessed in the UK*. WWT Report, Slimbridge.

Heath, M. F. & Evans, M.I. (eds.) 2000. *Important Bird Areas in Europe: Priority sites for conservation. 1: Northern Europe*. Cambridge, UK: Birdlife International (Birdlife Conservation Series No. 8).

Kershaw, M. & Cranswick, P.A. 2003. Numbers of wintering waterbirds in Great Britain, 1994/1995-1998/1999: I. Wildfowl and selected waterbirds. *Biological Conservation* 111: 91-104.

Kershaw, M., Hearn, R.D. & Cranswick, P.A. 2001. The role of ringing in integrated population monitoring of Anatidae in the United Kingdom. *Ardea* 89 (special issue): 209-220.

Kirby, J.S., Salmon, D.G., Atkinson-Willes, G.L. & Cranswick, P.A. 1995. Index numbers for waterbird populations, III. Long-term trends in the abundance of wintering wildfowl in Great Britain, 1966/67 to 1991/2. *Journal of Applied Ecology* 32: 536-551.

Kistchinski, A.A. & Vronski, N.V. 1979. On the summer distribution of *Branta bernicla bernicla*. In M.Smart (ed.) *Proceedings of the First Technical Meeting of Western Palearctic Migratory Bird Management*: 19-20. IWRB, Slimbridge.

Lack, P. 1986. *The Atlas of Wintering Birds in Britain and Ireland*. T. & A.D. Poyser, Calton.

Lambeck, R.H.D. 1990. Differences in migratory pattern and habitat choice between social classes of the Brent Goose *Branta b. bernicla*. *Ardea* 78: 426-440.

Lampio, T. 1979. Status of *Branta bernicla bernicla* in Finland. In: M. Smart (ed.) *Proceedings of the First Technical Meeting of Western Palearctic Migratory Bird Management*: 26-28. IWRB, Slimbridge.

Lovegrove, R., Williams, G. & Williams, I. 1994. *Birds in Wales*. Poyser, London.

Madsen, J. 1994. Dark-bellied Brent Geese in the Danish Wadden Sea: numbers and habitat utilisation. In: J. van Nugteren (ed.) *Brent Geese in the Wadden Sea*: 97-102. Dutch Society for the Preservation of the Wadden Sea, Leeuwarden.

Madge, S. & Burn, H. 1988. *Wildfowl: an identification guide to the ducks, geese and swans of the world*. Christopher Helm, London.

Maheo, R. 1994. Brent Geese in France. In J. van Nugteren, J. (ed.) *Brent Geese in the Wadden Sea*: 189-192. Dutch Society for the Preservation of the Wadden Sea, Leeuwarden.

Mansel-Pleydell, J.C. 1888. *The Birds of Dorsetshire*. Ballantyne Press, Edinburgh.

McKay, H.V., Bishop, J.D. & Ennis, D.C. 1994. The possible importance of nutritional requirements for Dark-bellied Brent Geese in the seasonal shift from winter cereals to pasture. *Ardea* 82: 123 –132.

McKay, H.V., Milsom, T.P., Feare, C.J. Ennis, D.C., O'Connell, D.P. & Haskell, D.J. 2001. Selection of forage species and the creation of alternative feeding areas for dark-bellied brent geese *Branta bernicla bernicla* in southern UK coastal areas. *Agriculture, Ecosystems and Environment* 84: 99-113.

Mitchell, C. & Ogilvie, M. 1997. Fifty years of wildfowl ringing by WWT. *Wildfowl* 47: 241-248.

Moser, M.E. 1988. Limits to the numbers of Grey Plover *Pluvialis squatarola* wintering on British estuaries: an analysis of long term population trends. *Journal of Applied Ecology* 25: 473-485.

Mullarney, K., Svensson, L., Zetterström, D. & Grant, P.J. 1999. *Collins Bird Guide*. HarperCollins, London.

Musgrove, A.J., Pollitt, M.S., Hall, C., Hearn, R.D., Holloway, S.J., Marshall, P.E., Robinson, J.A. & Cranswick, P.A. 2001. *The Wetland Bird Survey 1999-2000: Wildfowl and Wader Counts*. BTO/WWT/RSPB/JNCC, Slimbridge.

Nehls, H.W. 1979. Passage of *Branta bernicla bernicla* on the coast of the German Democratic Republic. In: M.Smart (ed.) *Proceedings of the First Technical Meeting of Western Palearctic Migratory Bird Management*: 33-36. IWRB, Slimbridge.

Owen, M., Atkinson-Willes, G.L. & Salmon, D.G. 1986. *Wildfowl in Great Britain*. Second edition. Cambridge University Press, Cambridge.

Payn, W. 1978. *The Birds of Suffolk*. Second edition. Ancient House Publishing, Ipswich.

Pollitt, M.S., Cranswick, P., Musgrove, A.J. Hall, C., Hearn, R.D., Robinson, J.A. & Holloway, S.J. 2000. *The Wetland Bird Survey 1998-99: Wildfowl and Wader Counts*. BTO/WWT/RSPB/JNCC, Slimbridge.

Potel, P. & Südbeck, P. 1994. Dark-bellied Brent Geese in Niedersachsen: a review of numbers, trends and distribution. In: J. van Nugteren (ed.) *Brent Geese in the Wadden Sea*: 87-96. Dutch Society for the Preservation of the Wadden Sea, Leeuwarden.

Prendergast, E.D.V. & Boys, J.V. 1983. *The Birds of Dorset*. David & Charles Ltd, Newton Abbot, Devon.

Prokosch, P. 1995. Mauser, Gewichte und Ringfunde von Ringelgänsen (*Branta bernicla bernicla*) auf Taimyr. In: P. Prokosch& H. Hötker (eds.) Faunistik und Naturschutz auf Taimyr - Expeditionen 1989-1991. *Corax* 16: 108-131.

Prop, J. 1997. Management and carrying capacity of salt marshes. In J. van Nugteren (ed.) *Dark-bellied Brent Goose Branta bernicla bernicla Flyway Management Plan*: 166-173. Coproduction IKC Natuurbeheer No. C-17. Information and Reference Cnetre for

Nature Management, Wageningen, The Netherlands.

Prŷs-Jones, R.P., Howells, R.J. & Kirby, J.S. 1989. *The abundance and distribution of wildfowl and waders on the Burry Inlet*. BTO Research Report 43. BTO, Thetford.

Prŷs-Jones, R.P., Underhill, L.G. & Waters, R.J. 1994. Index numbers for waterbird populations. II Coastal wintering waders in the United Kingdom, 1970/71 – 1990/91. *Journal of Applied Ecology* 31: 481-492.

Ramsar. 1999. *Strategic Framework for the List of Wetlands of International Importance*. Ramsar Bureau, Gland, Switzerland.

Ranwell, D.S. & Downing, B.M. 1959. Brent goose (*Branta bernicla* (L.)) winter feeding pattern and *Zostera* resources at Scolt Head Island, Norfolk. *Animal Behaviour* 7: 42-56.

Rose, P.M. & Scott, D.A. 1997. *Waterfowl Population Estimates – Second Edition*. Wetlands International Publ. 44, Wageningen, The Netherlands.

Rösner, H.U. & Stock, M. 1994. Numbers, recent changes, seasonal development and spatial distribution of Dark-bellied Brent Geese in Schleswig-Holstein. In: J. van Nugteren (ed.) *Brent Geese in the Wadden Sea*. Dutch Society for the Preservation of the Wadden Sea, Leeuwarden.

Rowcliffe, J.M. & Mitchell, C.R. 1998. *The conservation management of Brent Geese in the UK. Report to the Joint Nature Conservation Committee*. Wildfowl & Wetlands Trust Research Report, Slimbridge, UK.

Rowcliffe, J.M., Watkinson, A.R., Sutherland, W.J. and Vickery, J.A. 1995. Cyclic winter grazing patterns in Brent Geese and the regrowth of salt-marsh grass. *Functional Ecology* 9: 931-941.

Round, P. 1982. Inland feeding by Brent Geese *Branta bernicla* in Sussex, England. *Biological Conservation* 23: 15-32.

Salmon, D.G. & Fox, A.D. 1991. Dark-bellied Brent Geese *Branta bernicla bernicla* in Britain, 1976-1987. *Ardea* 79: 327-330.

Salomonsen, F. 1958. *The present status of the Brent Goose (*Branta bernicla *(L.)) in western Europe*. IWRB Publication 4.

Scott, D.A. & Rose P.M. 1996. *Atlas of Anatidae Populations in Africa and Western Eurasia*.

Wageningen, The Netherlands, Wetlands International Publication No. 44.

Shrubb, M. 1979. *The Birds of Sussex. Their Present Status*. Phillimore, London.

Smit, C.J. & Piersma, T. 1989. Numbers, mid-winter distribution, and migration of wader populations using the East Atlantic flyway. In: H. Boyd & J-Y. Pirot (eds.) *Flyways and reserve networks for water birds*: 24-63. International Waterfowl and Wetlands Research Bureau, Slimbridge.

Snow, D.W. & Perrins, C.M. 1998. *The Birds of the Western Palearctic Concise Edition*. Oxford University Press, Oxford.

Spaans, B., Stock, M., St.Joseph, A., Bergmann, H-H. & Ebbinge, B.S. 1993. Breeding biology of Dark-bellied Brent Geese *Branta b. bernicla* in Taimyr in 1990 in the absence of arctic foxes and under favourable weather conditions. *Polar Research* 12: 117-130.

Spaans, B., Bluleven, J., Popv, I., Rykhlikova, M.E. & Ebbinge, B.S. 1998. Dark-bellied Brent Geese *Branta bernicla bernicla* forgo breeding season when Arctic Foxes *Alopex lagopus* are present during nest initiation. *Ardea* 86: 11-20.

Stahl, J., Bos, D., & Loonen, M.J.J.E. 2002. Foraging along a salinity gradient – the effect of tidal inundation on site choice by Dark-belied Brent Geese *Branta bernicla* and Barnacle Geese *B.lecopsis*. *Ardea* 90: 201-212.

St Joseph, A.K.M. 1979a. The seasonal distribution and movement of *Brant bernicla* in western Europe. In: M. Smart (ed.) *Proceedings of the First Technical Meeting of Western Palearctic Migratory Bird Management*: 45-56. IWRB, Slimbridge.

St Joseph, A.K.M. 1979b. The development of inland feeding by *Branta bernicla bernicla* in southeastern England. In: M. Smart (ed.) *Proceedings of the First Technical Meeting of Western Palearctic Migratory Bird Management*: 132-139. IWRB, Slimbridge.

Stroud, D.A., Chambers, D., Cook, S., Buxton, N. Fraser, B., Clement, P., Lewis, I. McLean, I. Baker, H. & Whitehead, S. 2001. *The UK SPA network: its scope and content*. JNCC, Peterborough.

Summers, R.W. & Critchley, C.N.R. 1990. Use of grassland and field selection by brent geese *Branta bernicla*. *Journal of Applied Ecology* 27: 834-846.

Summers, R.W. & Hillman, G. 1990. Scaring Brent Geese *Branta b. bernicla* from fields of winter wheat with rape. *Crop Protection* 9: 459-35-37.

Summers, R.W. & Underhill, L.G. 1987. Factors related to breeding production of Brent Geese *Branta b. bernicla* and waders (Charadrii) on the Taimyr Peninsula. *Bird Study* 43: 161-171.

Summers, R.W. & Underhill, L.G. 1991. The growth of the population of Dark-bellied Geese *Branta b. bernicla* between 1955 and 1988. *Journal of Applied Ecology* 28: 574-585.

Summers, R.W., Underhill, L.G., Syroechkovski jnr, E.E., Lappo, H.G., Prŷs-Jones, R.P. & Karpov, V. 1994. The breeding biology of Dark-bellied Brent Geese *Branta b. bernicla* and King Eider *Somateria spectabilis* on the northeastern Taimyr Peninsula, especially in relation to Snowy Owl *Nyctea scandiaca* nests. *Wildfowl* 45: 110-118.

Summers, R.W., Underhill, L.G., Howells, R.J., Vickery, J.A. & Prŷs-Jones, R.P. 1996. Phenology of migration and use of wintering sites by the increasing population of dark-bellied geese *Branta bernicla bernicla. Journal of Zooogy. London* 239: 197-208.

Syroechkovsky, E.E. Jr. & Zoeckler, C. 1997. Eastern Black Brant mixes with western Dark-bellied Brent Goose in Yakutia. *Arctic Bulletin* 3: 16-17.

Underhill, L.G. & Prŷs-Jones, R.P. 1994. Index numbers for waterbird populations. 1. Review and Methodology. *Journal of Applied Ecology* 31: 463-480.

van Nugteren, J. (ed.) 1997. *Dark-bellied Brent Goose* Branta bernicla bernicla *Flyway Management Plan.* Coproduction IKC Natuurbeheer No. C-17. Information and Reference Cnetre for Nature Management, Wageningen, The Netherlands.

Vickery, J.A. & Summers, R.W. 1992. Cost-effectiveness of scaring Brent Geese *Branta b. bernicla* fromfields of arable crops by a human bird scarer. *Crop Protection* 11: 480-484.

Vinogradov, V.G. 1994. Changes in the Goose Status on the Kanin Peninsula. *IWRB Goose Research Group Bulletin* 5: 26-27.

Waters, R.J., Cranswick, P.A., Musgrove, A.J. & Pollitt, M.S. 1998. *The Wetland Bird Survey 1996-97 Wildfowl and Wader Counts.* BTO/WWT/RSPB/JNCC, Slimbridge.

Wetlands International. 2002. *Waterbird Population Estimates – Third Edition.* Wetlands International Global Series No. 12, Wageningen, The Netherlands.

White, R. & Webb, A. 1995. *Coastal birds and marine mammals of mid Dorset.* Joint Nature Conservation Committee, Peterborough.

White-Robinson, R. 1982. Inland and saltmarsh feeding of wintering Brent Geese in Essex. *Wildfowl* 33: 113-118.